When Elephants Die
How Conservatives Can Win The Presidency

John Jasek

When Elephants Die
How Conservatives Can Win The Presidency
Copyright © 2014 by John Jasek
All rights reserved.
ISBN-10: 1495900614
ISBN-13: 978-1495900617

Other books by the author: American Bondage: A Satire of Globalization

To INTPs and INTJs, analysts par excellence.

Preface

Four factors have led to the growing irrelevance of the national Republican Party: mass immigration, war, the 2008 economic crisis, and resolution of a philosophical argument.

The 1965 Immigration Act and a porous southern border have undermined the GOP. Republicans need look no further than the California State Assembly to see their own possible national fate.

America wasted trillions of dollars on credit card wars that resulted in thousands of American deaths and diminished America's standing in the world. Voters had no interest in permanent war and shunned the War Party in 2008 and 2012.

The 2008 financial crisis demonstrated that unrestrained capitalism means the Wall Street crapshoot, where insiders hoard America's wealth and working folks suffer. The Great Recession occurred against a backdrop of six million offshored jobs in the first decade of the century, gutting manufacturing in the name of corporate profits. Modest reshoring then took place under a Democratic president. The correlation in voters' minds between Republicans and offshoring, and Democrats and an industrial uptick, helped to ensure Republican defeat in Election 2012.

"Small government" has come to mean protecting corporate interests at the expense of social justice for the middle and working classes. Voters want social programs, not entitlements for the wealthy. The argument over government has been settled. "Small government" lost.

Few predicted the collapse of Marxist regimes in Central and Eastern Europe. 9/11 came out of the blue. The American government was blind-sided by the 2008 financial crisis and the deep recession that followed. The Arab Spring caught people by surprise. Such volatility, and the high probability that financial predators will again bring misery to America, and will again go unpunished, will ensure demand for an extensive social welfare net.

The contradiction of "small government"/globalist philosophy is that it created conditions that made larger government inevitable as millions of middle and working class Americans became economically disenfranchised.

"Small government" + globalization + finance capitalism = government moving in to salvage what it can. "Small government" could no more benefit the people in the paradigm of a casino or the global plantation than oranges could be grown on the Arctic tundra. The Republican Party supported policies that made marginalization of the GOP inevitable.

With Republicans unable or unwilling to veer from destruction, conservatives should create a new party that combines realism with vision. It will have to stand with American workers, not investment bankers and corporate executives. Or realist conservatives can take control of the GOP, ending its suicide fetish.

Adherence to irrational ideology prevents the GOP from adopting logical choices for survival.

Republicans believe their message is fine when Election Day reality demonstrates otherwise.

Contempt for reason and evidence has gotten the GOP nowhere. It's been said the definition of insanity is repeating the same thing over and over and expecting a different outcome. That outcome won't change unless conservatives try something different.

Chapter 1
Self-destruction

Election 2012 was the GOP's for the taking. Republicans chose not to, snatching defeat from the jaws of victory. Instead of offering a program to help working people, the GOP opted to learn nothing from the past, nothing from failure.

President Obama won, not because his policies were stellar, for the economy was not, but because the GOP's election platform was unpalatable to most voters. The result was predictable: an eminently beatable president was easily reelected. A president who led the country during a time of high unemployment, who added trillions to the national debt, and who presided over anemic economic growth, won big.

If Republicans couldn't win in 2012, when can they win? And how? Who will vote for them? The GOP has no credibility when it speaks of winning Latino voters when it has problems winning white working class voters in Ohio, Pennsylvania, Michigan, Wisconsin, Minnesota, and Washington. In the aftermath of the steepest economic downturn since the Great Depression, millions of white Americans chose to stay home rather than cast a ballot on Election Day.

There is an air of fantasy to GOP talk of a Latino strategy when Republicans don't even have a European American strategy. Republicans struggle with white ethnics and the northern white working class. They get modest support from single white women, gay white men, and northern whites making under $30,000 a year. Whites in a dozen northern states vote for the Democratic presidential candidate or give the Republican candidate a narrow victory. And the GOP wants to win over Latinos? Republicans can't even win Maine.

It won't get easier for Republicans going forward. Demographic trends are against them. Demographic change is more responsible for the GOP's existential crisis than any other factor.

Obama's first term foreign policy was successful enough. He brought home U.S. troops from Iraq and began winding down U.S. involvement in Afghanistan. He refused to drag America into war with Iran.

Of the many acts of self-sabotage the GOP has committed, becoming the War Party in the eyes of the American public was one that could easily have been avoided. When faced with this obvious trap, the Republican Party chose to dive right into it.

Under Bush 43, a conflict begun to punish the man most responsible for 9/11 turned into a protracted general war. When Osama bin Laden was finally found, he wasn't even in Afghanistan.

The war against Iraq was based on fallacies from the get-go. No weapons of mass destruction, no terror plots, little to justify America's intervention in that country. Ousting a tyrant was a good thing, but Iraq is today divided along sectarian lines, and Iraq's ancient Christian community is less than half its pre-war size.

Iran is often described by neocons as a country a few years away from possessing nuclear weapons, and they've been saying it for 20 years.

When given an opportunity for a foreign policy reset that would have allowed the GOP to renounce a discredited neoconservative past, top Republicans endorsed air strikes against Syria. Russia schooled the GOP on foreign policy by proposing Syrian chemical weapons come under international control. Russia was the winner. Obama came across as reasonable if bumbling by walking back on air strikes. Prominent Republicans took the rope by supporting air strikes and were left hanging, coming across as inane when Obama backpedalled.

Instead of going into Election 2016 with foreign policy credibility, or credibility on much of anything, the GOP comes across as inept. Then why vote for them? The question Republicans should ask themselves is this: How is the GOP different from Democrats in ways that don't alienate the white working class? Now count up these differences to see if they make for a winning election platform. Verify the answer by checking the results of the last two presidential elections. Simple math.

The 2012 presidential election saw the Republican Party all but fade into history as a serious contender on America's national political stage. The Party of Lincoln might regain the Oval Office once or twice more before the final nail is pounded into the GOP's coffin, but the window for such theatricality is small and will be slammed shut within a decade or so. That "Democratic fatigue" might be the best bet for a future GOP term at the White House indicates how far the Republican Party has fallen. It's possible that 2004 will be the answer to a future trivia question: When was the last time the Republican Party won the White House?

If Democrats become Oval Office fixtures in coming decades, they'll likely move further to the left to be more in sync with priorities of the Democratic Party's base. Left-wing justices would then preside over the Supreme Court, ending the political balance of the judicial branch of government. Congress would resemble a rubber-stamp parliament.

A nationally viable conservative party is essential if America is to maintain political equilibrium. Not achieving that balance in a country so diverse will only exacerbate societal divisions. A de facto American one-party state would make a mockery of everything America claims to be and the country would be unable to be taken seriously as a democracy.

The paradox of a poor economy during Obama's first term was that it helped Democrats. Voters looked at the alternative and decided things could be worse. People cringed at the prospect of returning to how things were under Bush 43, when the casino wrought the Great Recession and good jobs were disappearing by the millions.

There exists a Democratic Firewall of northern industrial states of the GOP's making. That barrier exists because of Republican policies. The GOP has remained tone deaf to the hurt of Middle America, opting instead to remain tight with Wall Street.

Anger directed at America's financial sector and a rigged economy runs deep and won't dissipate soon. Why? Because the anger is justified and an economic system designed to make the rich richer, come what may, remains in place. America's economic structure benefits insiders at the expense of outsiders, rewards Wall Street and punishes Main Street. A system of privatized gains and socialized losses for yacht owners is no model for fairness and prosperity.

As both parties have churned out pro-Wall Street administrations, Republicans and Democrats should be equally susceptible to voter wrath, but the GOP has played matters so poorly, with little grasp of working folk sensibilities, that all Democrats had to do was let Republicans speak.

One or two changes to the GOP's platform might have made for a different outcome in Election 2012: a tax hike on the wealthy, a wealth tax on individuals worth more than $50 million, tariffs, an increase in the minimum wage, higher corporate taxes on American companies that offshore, a realist foreign policy.

Republicans had to do something, anything, to make northern working class voters want to vote for them in numbers sufficient to win the White House. It never happened. The GOP candidate never set himself apart from the dogma of his own party.

What happened after the election? In negotiations over the so-called fiscal cliff, the GOP caved on taxes with the top tax rate increasing from 35% to 39.6%. This raises the question: If Republicans were going to cave on a tax hike for the wealthy, why didn't they do it before the election when they had the chance to win working class voters in Ohio and Pennsylvania? A strategy of flip-flop and capitulation shows a rudderless party, careening from crisis to crisis, refusing to behave rationally.

The GOP's political fortunes depend largely on Democrat failure: an Obamacare disaster, foreign policy debacle, or a weak economy. Republicans have done little to help their own cause. Obamacare is a prime example. House Republicans spent years opposing it before coming up with their own alternative plan — the American Healthcare Reform Act — *after* the 2012 election. What was the point of unveiling a plan *after* the election? Did the GOP think being the *Party of No* would win them the White House?

Republicans repeatedly shoot themselves in the foot and at times can't seem to get anything right. During the 2013 government shutdown, Republicans opposed raising the debt ceiling, and then promptly caved. They failed to defund the Affordable Care Act. Then what was the point of the government shutdown? What was the strategy? Why deflect attention from the rollout of Obamacare?

Demographic woes aside, the GOP will face more difficulties than Democrats in winning the White House. If the economy improves, few will want to go back to the way things were under Bush 43. If the economy weakens, voters might prefer more government help, and not neocon nostrums.

"Small government" has effectively become a code term, applied punitively to the middle and working classes, with neocons railing about the cost of social programs, while investment bankers are bailed out and insiders are protected. As long as the Wall Street-Washington Axis exists, "small government" won't be a vote-winning philosophy.

Government's purpose must be to stand with Main Street. Millions of U.S. jobs were sent overseas in the 2000s. Neocons like to say it's not the role of government to interfere in the "free market," but a

GOP administration did just that to bail out Wall Street. The rules of the market in neocon eyes apply only to the poor.

"Small government" and the "free market" are so tainted by hypocrisy that conservatives should stop using the terms on the campaign trail.

For conservatism to become a viable alternative to the left, conservatives must advocate moderate and effective government. To defend tax breaks for the rich and bailouts for Wall Street is to remain irrelevant. To act as if offshoring is as American as apple pie is to be irrational. Conservatives need to win Main Street. They're not going to do that by sucking up to investment bankers, hedge fund managers, and corporate tycoons.

Anatomy of a Suicide

Why, then, does the Republican Party support policies designed to bring about its own extinction? Dogma is the main reason. Just as Soviet Marxist ideologues once espoused proletarian internationalism when the example of the world proved it silly, so too do neocons champion free trade and the Wall Street casino, even when it leads to Republican ruin.

In a country whose culture is infused with an aversion to finance capitalism and "small government," the GOP is flailing against the zeitgeist. Class warfare works, and it works because the working class has been hurting. If economic discrepancies were not so prominent, class warfare would fall on deaf ears.

Republicans don't speak to working class voters as working class voters. Instead, the GOP offers gobbledygook about how lowering taxes for the rich will create jobs and lower deficits. Republicans might as well ask voters to form a magic circle and chant, "trickle down."

If government could authorize hundreds of billions for the Troubled Asset Relief Program so the Wall Street casino could be stabilized, surely it made sense to help the 99 percent of people who didn't get rich from the casino and not view that assistance as a drain on society. Where is the logic in helping investment bankers and then opposing long-term unemployment benefits for workers caught in a steep recession caused by the same investment bankers government refused to regulate adequately?

Quantitative easing has seen government pump trillions of dollars into the stock market so that the market could set record highs and the rich could recoup losses from the Great Recession. Yet again the wealthy were coddled. Wall Street has become America's largest welfare program.

To then focus on unemployment benefits or food stamps is irrational. House Republicans showed callousness by voting to cut $40 billion from food stamps over ten years. Such a cut would deprive food assistance to millions of people, many of them white and poor and living in what are now red states. SNAP has helped millions and has benefited the economy by increasing grocery store business. To cut food stamps assistance to people struggling to get by will only hurt the GOP in many swing states.

Republican politicians should be more concerned about ending Wall Street welfare than cutting food assistance to red state voters. The problem is with the Wall Street-Washington Axis, with corporate and political elites, not with the working poor or a struggling middle class.

If neoconservatives are determined to create a corporate paradise where American workers are left with low-paying jobs, then it's government's duty to increase the minimum wage and provide an extensive social welfare net.

But every four years the GOP presidential candidate does little more than strut the voodoo economics dance of a globalist witch doctor. He lurches from state to state, carrying a bag filled with snake oil. Republicans then wonder why they have problems.

Conservatives have a chance to create a contract with American workers, where creating good-paying jobs and a strong middle class are held in higher regard than fealty to the casino and globalization. They have an opportunity to reassert that the United States is a country and not a shopping mall, and that Americans are citizens and not economic units.

For what is the purpose of conservatism other than to conserve — a people, economy, and culture? If American conservatives aren't up to this most basic of tasks, which politicians in non-Western societies do as naturally as breathing, what is the point of having an American conservative party at all?

Chapter 2
IDEOLOGY

Few Republicans ask how someone who was arguably the most unvetted person to become president in modern times could have been elected not once, but twice. And it doesn't seem to occur to Republicans who ask the question that the answer is found by looking in the mirror.

Obama was able to win the presidency twice because his economic platform came across as more reasonable than the Republican one. Although media and academic elites lean to the left, Obama was not as economically liberal a president as some of his detractors painted him out to be. Did the Obama administration preside over a 90 percent income tax rate on the wealthiest Americans, as the Eisenhower administration did? Was Obama more economically liberal than LBJ or Nixon?

To his credit, Obama helped vulnerable elements of society during the Great Recession, and in his second term, unemployment and the deficit started to fall significantly for the first time in years.

Most Americans don't want utopia for the rich and corporations. Nor do most Americans want the United States constantly at war. For a party that boasts that it understands business, the Republican Party doesn't do a good job of selling itself in presidential elections.

Neoconservatives espouse a corporate globalist destiny for America, a capitalist version of proletarian internationalism. But the neoconservative version of the end of history is a protest against realism, for neocon control of the GOP is leading the Republican Party to its end with history.

TYPES OF CONSERVATISM

Neocons might as well posit that transglobal oligarchs should have a standing in society similar to the divine right of kings and should then be allowed to throw American workers under the bus. Oh wait...

Conservatives build. They construct, not deconstruct and destruct. As neoconservatism is the antithesis of conservatism, conservatives should work to change the current GOP. If the Republican Party doesn't change, conservatives should push for change in a new party.

Conservatives should pick and choose strands from different parts of the conservative spectrum, forming a message relevant to today's realities.

Paleoconservatism

Paleoconservatives shun neoconservative and liberal utopias. They favor realist foreign policy, moderate immigration, and believe government shouldn't spend more money than it takes in. They oppose free trade and bailing out Wall Street, being more interested in a viable middle class than in adding to the wealth of corporate executives and investment bankers. Paleocons support a night-watchman state.

Progressive Conservatism

Progressive conservatives favor progressive tax policies, government funding for infrastructure, and broad-based social welfare. Such views are little in evidence in today's GOP.

Social Conservatism

Some supposed social conservative tenets, the sanctity of family, for example, are to be lauded. But social liberals also value family. Social conservatives do not have a monopoly on being pro-family.

But there is something socially conservative about denigrating gay folks and gay relationships. Some social conservatives advocate discrimination against LGBT Americans, going so far as labeling gays perverse and immoral. So which group is more pro-family — social conservatives or social liberals?

Even if homosexuality constituted abnormal behavior, how would it be more odd than chain-smoking, alcoholism, gambling, and divorce — failings that afflict many heterosexuals? Why, then, don't social conservatives obsess about chain smokers, alcoholics, and divorced men?

This sort of hypocrisy has attenuated social conservatism, making it increasingly irrelevant. It's important conservatives focus on economic issues and existential matters, not fixate over two men wanting to get hitched at city hall.

State Capitalism

State capitalism is today most often associated with China, Japan, Taiwan, South Korea, and Singapore. It involves some degree of government control, but not ownership, of industry. Some laissez faire advocates argue that Beijing has created a financial bubble that will bring havoc to China, as if laissez faire America hasn't had its own financial bubbles.

It's impossible to deny the speed and scale of China's modernization. Whatever weaknesses state capitalism has, it also has its strengths. State capitalism is a model America should partially emulate to power its economy in this century.

Libertarianism

Libertarianism is sometimes categorized as a type of conservatism, or at least closer to conservatism than to contemporary liberalism, but its economic version is a form of anarchism. The libertarian view of the world is the market is magical and the state will wither away.

As an economic model, libertarianism constitutes mumbo jumbo. Libertarians want to eliminate income tax, but offer no way of paying for federal programs. A common response: get rid of federal programs. Not exactly a vote winner.

Reverence for globalism further undermines economic libertarianism. It's hard to believe anyone would want to empower Wall Street and corporations more than they've already been empowered in America, but libertarians believe there should be no minimum wage, no borders, few regulations on the casino, few if any limits on free trade or immigration.

Privatization is a key libertarian tenet, but it would be silly for government departments to compete against private sector rivals so that there are 5 defense departments, 7 commerce departments, and 19 state departments fighting amongst each other for business, and it would be pointless for cities to have multiple fire and police departments offering services. Libertarianism = economic lunacy.

But libertarians do have some good non-economic ideas. Libertarians value civil liberty. Unlike some liberals, libertarians believe in free speech, not just left-wing speech.

To their credit, many libertarians opposed Sections 1021 and 1022 of the 2012 version of the National Defense Authorization Act, which allowed for indefinite military detention without trial of U.S. citizens.

Libertarians have practical views on social issues. Many libertarians favor legalizing gay marriage and prostitution. They advocate a harm-reduction strategy for drug addicts, which is more sensible than arresting addicts and classifying them as criminals. Drug addicts are not criminals and shouldn't be treated as such. The noxious smell of marijuana justifies prohibiting pot from being smoked in public, but it should not be a crime for adults to smoke it at home or in a secluded outdoor space.

Like paleocons, libertarians favor a non-interventionist approach to world affairs, not preemption and permanent conflagration.

Conclusion

To win the presidency, conservatives need to look across the political spectrum, picking what works, disregarding what doesn't. America needs a conservative party that supports evidence-based solutions, not pixie dust or dogma or a Hail Mary pass. And that party needs to keep an eye on its own survival. If it can't do that, it won't exist for long.

Chapter 3
Existential Dilemma

GOP Suicide Watch

Immigration has contributed to American exceptionalism. It has helped to create a dynamic society of people with different talents, experiences, and life views. All the more ironic, then, that more than anything else, mass immigration could result in the end of a two-party system that has provided equilibrium to American politics since the 19th Century.

Immigration to the United States has grown from 250,000 immigrants per year in the 1950s, to 450,000 per annum in the 1970s, to 730,000 per year in the 1980s, to almost 1 million people now. But over the decades, whenever Americans were asked if they wanted immigration decreased, to remain at current levels, or increased substantially, the last option had little public support. Yet Washington chose the last option every time. Many Democrats and Republicans on Capitol Hill want to increase immigration yet again and give amnesty to more than ten million people.

America is no longer a frontier country in need of settlers or an early industrial society in need of nation builders, but a republic of hundreds of millions of people. Immigration is all but woven into America's DNA, but with deindustrialization, globalism, and technology rapidly changing the dynamics of work and wages in the United States, selective immigration makes more sense than mass immigration.

U6 unemployment has remained in double digits for years. Many of the jobs created since the end of the Great Recession have been low-wage, part-time jobs that allow for bare subsistence. Bringing in tens of millions of immigrants in the span of barely more than a generation under these conditions is unlikely to benefit those at the lower end of the economic ladder.

How has mass immigration helped the American working class over the last 30 years? If there's been no benefit, by what logic does one assume that American workers will benefit from much higher levels of mass immigration over the next 30 years? And if the overall effect of mass immigration over the past three decades has been neutral, or negative, then why more mass immigration?

An AI and robot revolution could result in large-scale unemployment in coming years. At the time of this writing, robots can harvest crops and make hamburgers in restaurants. Skilled and unskilled jobs will increasingly become automated.

It's conceivable that productivity gains made possible by machines will allow for an extensive social safety net, but it's too early to say whether robots and AI will create more opportunities for man than they take away. And if machines do make human work less common, even redundant in many cases, why mass immigration?

Neocons and liberals accept as gospel that mass immigration benefits society. Yet countries prosper with minimal immigration. Homogenous European nation-states attract immigrants precisely because these societies have attained high living standards.

And until recently, many of these countries had few social and economic divisions.

Finland and Denmark have no resources save the industry and intelligence of their peoples. America, by contrast, has vast natural resources and has been on an immigration binge for half a century. Yet the quality of life in America is not better than in Finland or Denmark.

Japan and many European countries file more patents per million people than an America that has accepted 40 million immigrants over the last 50 years. But such an outcome goes against neocon dogma. Then why adhere to the dogma?

Those who argue mass immigration is needed to counter the effects of an aging society often ignore the fact that immigrants get old. More immigrants would then be needed and then more and more. There's a term for this sort of thing. Oh wait...

Where is the evidence that mass immigration makes a country more cohesive than a country with minimal immigration? How does mass immigration improve living standards and reduce socioeconomic divisions in a country? Could it be that large-scale immigration makes a country less cohesive than a country with moderate or minimal immigration? Then why mass immigration? Could socioeconomic divisions in society increase as the result of mass immigration? If so, then why mass immigration?

It's been oft repeated that immigration has helped to make America a culturally vibrant society. But how much immigration does a country need to be "vibrant?" Japan, South Korea, and Vietnam are culturally vibrant as are Finland, Germany, Australia,

Denmark, and Poland. These countries have experienced different rates of immigration, some a bit, some more, and some a lot. Yet all are culturally "vibrant." America even managed to win the Second World War, put a man on the moon, and reach its apex as an economic power versus the world during an immigration lull.

As this book is about the demise of the Republican Party, the crux of the matter is this: *Mass immigration + a stagnant middle and working class = a bad place for the GOP.* To a large extent, the Republican Party has been brought to its precarious state by immigration and economic policies championed by the GOP. Most Republicans refuse to admit to this, but that's irrelevant. What's relevant is reality.

Mass immigration, deindustrialization, and automation exist alongside a low American minimum wage, which would have to almost double to provide basic economic security and the dignity that comes with it. Someone who has gone from working on the factory floor at a decent wage to working in retail at minimum wage and barely surviving is unlikely to vote for a Republican candidate. And for decades the GOP has done poorly with Latino immigrants and their descendants in presidential elections.

In other words, the Republican Party is faced with a two-pronged takedown. Journalists have written extensively about the impact of America's growing Latino population on the GOP. Economic difficulties faced by northern whites are a less discussed factor in GOP decline. Poor and middle class northern whites vote in large numbers for the Democratic Party, yet the GOP needs to win these voters to win the presidency.

Republicans should try to increase their share of the Latino vote by supporting amnesty, but also try to win increased support of northern whites by calling for a higher minimum wage, tariffs, and other pro-worker measures.

And as most Americans support moderate immigration, it makes sense to support amnesty while advocating lower overall immigration levels. Republicans should support bringing in modest numbers of specialists, not hundreds of thousands of additional low-skilled workers each year.

Few conservatives and moderates can fathom why so many Republicans support immigration reform proposals that would put more stress on American workers by increasing competition for low wage jobs. What is the point in doing this? And how would vastly increasing low-skilled immigration do anything other than hurt the Republican Party?

By supporting dramatically increased immigration, the GOP not only stands to the left of the American people, but it does nothing to position itself as an alternative to the Democrats. *Question for Republicans: Why should working class voters support a party that wants to increase greatly immigration levels, supports free trade, and opposes raising the minimum wage?*

Immigration reform is a minefield for Republicans. Few believe that a party that has repeatedly snatched defeat from the jaws of victory can navigate that minefield. To sign off on yet another amnesty after the debacle that was the Simpson-Mazzoli Act would be humiliation and embarrassment enough for the GOP, but any new amnesty would quickly descend to the level of farce for Republicans if the GOP keeps going the way of the Dodo in presidential elections.

The Republican Party is trapped in a Catch-22. The GOP should sign off on amnesty, and yes, it would be amnesty not some euphemism, but the moment the Republican Party does so it announces to the world that it has been inept for decades, and that it has caved yet again to the Democrats. It would be a signing ceremony of defeat. There would no way to spin it otherwise. Then comes the question: Why should the Republican Party exist?

Ignoring the Evidence

The GOP acts as if it's only a matter of time before Latinos vote en masse for the Republican Party. But why would Latinos do so? Mexican Americans drop out of high school at a higher rate than whites and experience a higher poverty rate than European Americans. Poor Mexican Americans aren't going to vote for a party that believes government is the problem. And if wage growth remains uneven, it might only be a matter of time until poor whites abandon the GOP in droves.

Some neoconservatives opine affluence will make Latinos more Republican. Where is the evidence for this? Middle class Mexican Americans vote for the Democratic Party. Through what oracle of divination have neoconservatives been informed this will change? And how will neocons turn poor Latinos into GOP voters?

Some social conservatives say Mexican Americans are natural Republican voters because Mexican Americans are big on "family values." Which ethnic group isn't big on "family values?" White ethnics are big on "family values," but split their vote with the majority opting for Democrats in recent presidential contests. English-American Mormons and southern British Americans are also big on "family values," but vote by a substantial margin for the GOP.

Why isn't every group voting in the majority for the Republican Party if "family values" are the key to presidential victory and if the Republican Party embodies those values? Was bailing out Wall Street part of some "family values" program? Republicans don't have to look far to see why their "family values" agenda hasn't been a winner.

Individuals from ethnic groups culturally distinct from the majority are more likely to vote along ethnic lines for Democrats than individuals from populations more closely aligned to Anglo-American culture. This is America's voting reality. This is what the evidence shows. Why does the GOP want to replace evidence with wishful thinking in its political calculations?

The idea that the solution to the GOP's Latino problem is to import tens of millions more future Democratic Party voters, in other words to keep doing what got the GOP into its demographic/electoral predicament in the first place, is irrational. The evidence indicates this will solidify a Democratic majority. The 1965 Immigration Act and a previous amnesty haven't benefited the Republican Party. The GOP won't be rejuvenated by more mass immigration.

For Republicans to win more Latino voters, the GOP will have to adopt a centrist economic agenda.

Logic and the evidence must drive policymaking, not fantasy, wishful thinking, or political theory. One can't help but think of Soviet communists, who thought that if only they delved into Marx's writings deep enough, all problems would be surmounted. Neocons are as deluded, for they refuse to accept reality.

The difficulty Republicans will have in getting Latinos, northern whites, and conservatives to vote for the Republican Party in presidency winning numbers should not be underestimated. Republicans will have to find a way to finesse their policies so that they can make inroads with pro-amnesty Latinos without alienating conservatives and independents.

The GOP will also have to find a way to win over northern voters who support progressive economics, oppose war, despise free trade, and are skeptical of amnesty. It's a lot of hoops to jump through. That the GOP is consistently unable to win Ohio, Michigan, Pennsylvania, Wisconsin, Oregon, and other northern states only demonstrates how inept the Republican Party has become in presidential contests.

An (Almost) Impossible Mess

Conservatives should support amnesty for those who were brought to America illegally at a young age and who've met DREAM Act requirements. This could be offset by cuts to legal immigration going forward.

Amnesty for 11 million illegal immigrants without add-on legislation to help American workers will pose challenges for the Republican Party that the GOP won't be able to overcome. Ronald Reagan signed into law the 1986 Simpson-Mazzolli Act. Latinos have voted in the majority for the Democratic candidate in presidential election after presidential election since then, as they had for decades before 1986.

Amnesty could mean employment competition for the white working class, which might become more solidified in opposing any "small government" philosophy that seeks to take away social benefits. In other words, more white Americans might become Democratic voters.

The costs of amnesty could be substantial: millions would become eligible for social programs. So long as decent-paying jobs are available, these costs should be manageable as most people want to work, but the economy has only recently showed signs of strength after years of sluggishness.

Legalized illegal immigrants would also become eligible for affirmative action programs denied to the white working class. Do Republicans not get how weird that would be?

If amnesty is enacted and its costs are extensive, will Republicans at some future date use those costs as an excuse to propose limiting social programs for all, thereby punishing American workers for the GOP's support of amnesty? Neocons might actually believe such a stance would appeal to working class voters. Oh wait...

Even a short analysis of amnesty and immigration reform indicates a large number of pitfalls for the GOP with few such problems for the Democratic Party. So why take on so much risk when one is likely to lose anyway? Because the GOP doesn't have much choice and because it's still possible for Republicans to win increased Latino and European American support by supporting a deft combination of immigration and economic reform.

Mexico has been the top source of legal immigrants to America for decades and Mexico will remain a major source of legal immigrants for the foreseeable future. Mexican Americans have helped to build America, placing their cultural imprint on American society, like the Italians, Poles, Irish, and Germans have done.

An open and optimistic paradigm of assimilation is a cultural strength of the United States. In this sense, America has an advantage over Europe, which is much divided over immigration, and over East Asia, where immigration is viewed with such distaste that it's barely permitted.

The GOP's existential crisis stems from the sheer number of legal and illegal immigrants to the United States over the last 40 years. It would be political suicide for Republicans to agree to amnesty without the border first having been secured and without higher wages for American workers having been guaranteed.

Outreach to bring more Latinos into the GOP is important, but so is outreach to bring in more white ethnic voters, white working class voters, white women, and gay white men. Republicans need to win the North as much as they need to win the South.

To gain support from disparate groups, the Republican Party should *supplement* immigration reform with legislation to help American workers, which *might* result in more Latinos voting for the GOP, *plus* help the GOP with northern working class voters. No guarantees, but Republicans have made such a mess of things that they can't expect guarantees. *The Republican Party has to prove that it's interested in helping America's working and middle classes.*

And unless Republicans modify their economic agenda, most Mexican Americans will likely continue voting for the Democratic candidate in presidential elections. Many Republican backers of amnesty are advocating eventual citizenship for as many as 15 or 20 million people, including family members of the legalized. Do Republicans understand what this would mean for GOP political fortunes? Do Republican strategists have any grasp of reality?

But a vast class of illegal immigrants is not good for America. Second, it is neither practical nor moral to deport 11 million people. All other considerations aside, amnesty is the morally correct thing to do, whatever the impact on the GOP. Third, America is partly to blame for the mess. To blame illegal immigrants for U.S. government negligence is hardly right. Fourth, amnesty won't stop marginalization of the GOP. The decline of the GOP was begun decades ago and Republicans have been unapologetically complicit in it.

It was never in the national interest to allow 11 million illegal immigrants into the United States. That it was allowed to happen speaks to Democratic and Republican irresponsibility. But it has happened. *Some sort of amnesty will happen, sooner or later. Then why should conservatives not do it in a way to maximize conservative advantage?*

By supporting progressive conservative economic policies, the Republican Party would not only win increased support from working class whites, but would also increase its share of the Latino vote. And whose support would the GOP lose? Corporate types, Wall Street types, and ideological cranks for the most part. The party would lose few genuine small government supporters, as most of these folks are smart enough to realize that helping the rich doesn't translate to favoring small government. Many such voters left the GOP years ago. Some vote Libertarian, some Democrat and many stay at home. In short, the GOP would win more voters than they would lose, many more.

Link immigration reform to pro-worker legislation, not corporate interests

No political party should favor corporations over the working class and poor. Haven't corporations already been given enough, far more than enough? And why hurt the people whose votes you need to win the White House? It gives *ruce to the bottom* an entirely new meaning.

Conservatives should advocate an immediate $11 an hour minimum wage, rising to $14 an hour over four years. Conservative insistence on a $14 minimum wage would force Democrats to agree, or not. If Democrats disagree, the conversation becomes one of treating American workers fairly. Conservatives win. If Democrats agree, conservatives still get increased support from the working class. Then they campaign in Michigan, Ohio, and Pennsylvania.

Democrats are almost certain to make a hike in the minimum wage a major campaign issue in 2016. It would be a mistake for the GOP to support amnesty and oppose the Democrats on raising the minimum wage. It would be the perfect setup for Republican failure. How many times does the GOP want to snatch defeat from the jaws of victory? Why not take the issue off the table in a stroke by telling working class Americans in Ohio and Michigan that they deserve to be better paid? Democratic and Republican voters, as well as independents, support a hike in the minimum wage. *Raising the minimum wage to $14 an hour over several years should be a basic requirement of amnesty.*

A minimum wage increase would benefit America's working poor. And neocons can stop with their "raising the minimum wage increases unemployment" refrain. Washington, for example, has a minimum wage well above the national one and the state's unemployment rate is below the national unemployment rate.

A higher minimum wage means higher employee retention rates in service and retail jobs. It means companies save money on job training. It benefits employers and employees. Workers would have more income to spend on products, which in turn would create more jobs. Only the people getting more money would include poorer folks. Now there's a novel idea. It's *trickle up,* not *trickle down.* It's a win-win situation for all.

The minimum wage would be almost $11 today had it kept pace with the U.S. rate of inflation since 1968. The U.S. unemployment rate in 1968 was under 4%. Had the minimum wage kept pace with productivity gains since 1968, it would be more than $14 an hour today. Where is the evidence that an immediate minimum wage hike to $11 would significantly inflate prices or result in higher unemployment?

A $14 minimum wage would mean social program spending could fall, reducing the tax burden on working class taxpayers and also lowering the deficit and debt. Equivalent costs of social programs would be transferred from the working and middle classes to corporations in the form of a living wage. Now there's a private sector approach that neoconservatives should support, isn't it? Oh wait...Wall Street wouldn't be happy. *The main thing is that Main Street be happy. That's all conservatives should be thinking about. The starting point is American workers, not corporations.* The GOP seems unable to grasp this.

If it's not conservative to almost double the minimum wage, by what logic is it conservative to keep wages low while giving amnesty to more than ten million people who entered the United States unlawfully? It's not conservative at all, but it's so very neocon.

If mass immigration = a big plus for American workers, increase the minimum wage. A rule of thumb should be the more government increases immigration, the higher the minimum wage should be. Liberals and neocons often state that bringing in tens of millions of immigrants over the next couple of decades will benefit America's working class. They say that mass immigration does not adversely affect low-wage American workers, and that wage suppression is myth. Maybe they're right, in which case why oppose hiking the minimum wage to a modest $14 over a four-year timeframe?

Economic liberals, at least, back up their view that mass immigration is a good thing by supporting a substantial minimum wage hike for American workers. This gives them an inherent advantage over GOP advocates of amnesty. Do neocons think they've developed a winning election strategy by keeping wages low for American workers while increasing immigration?

Which groups(s) do neocons expect to excite with talk of ever-higher levels of immigration, free trade, "enterprise zones," low wages, war, and by being all chummy with Wall Street bankers? Neocons have created a fictional demographic, a voting bloc that does not exist.

Extending unemployment benefits for unemployed Americans to at least three years should also be a requirement for amnesty. If amnesty has a positive effect on wages and employment, then unemployment will fall and there will be money for the remaining unemployed.

A third requirement for amnesty is securing the border. Not doing so is an affront to rational governance. The border should have been secured 40 years ago.

Fourth, as a matter of basic social justice, put in place affirmative action programs for white ethnics and poor Anglo-Americans. Such programs should be considered mandatory if tens of millions of new immigrants are to be added to the labor market and if they and their progeny are to be eligible for affirmative action for generations to come.

Fifth, impose tariffs on foreign goods to expedite an American manufacturing surge.

Return to Realism

If mass immigration leads to national prosperity, both parties should support almost doubling the minimum wage before almost doubling immigration. If mass immigration is not an elixir, go forward with amnesty, but cut immigration to 200,000-400,000 immigrants a year for a generation, which *might* put upward pressure on wages over time. Allow labor mobility between Canada and the United States, and increase the minimum wage to $14 an hour over four years.

Labor mobility between Canada and America once existed and labor mobility is the norm between most countries of the EU. Free movement of workers also occurs between Australia and New Zealand. Labor mobility between Canada and America would likely involve a modest circular immigrant flow that would benefit both countries.

Republicans should take a common sense view of immigration instead of wanting to almost double it. Why accept an approach to immigration that benefits corporations, Wall Street bankers, and real estate speculators undeniably, but whose effects on the working class are uncertain or detrimental?

Conservatives will have to find a way to pick two electoral/demographic locks, a Democratic Northern Firewall of Ohio, Pennsylvania, Michigan, Wisconsin, Minnesota, New England, Washington, and Oregon, and a Southern Lock, one which didn't exist three decades ago, but which now bolts shut California, and will soon keep the Republican Party from winning Arizona, Florida, Texas, Virginia, Nevada, and North Carolina.

Conservatives should support moderate immigration, fair tax policies, tariffs, a higher minimum wage, and a welfare state. Doing so might not make a difference in conservative fortunes at this point. Demographic change has been so massive and rapid that the GOP could be in a quandary for which the only solution is the fracturing of the Democratic Party or the emergence of a third party.

Realistically, perhaps the only way to get white Americans and Latinos to vote for a conservative party in the numbers needed to put a conservative in the White House is for conservatives to support moderate government and moderate immigration.

Question, again, for the GOP: Why should it support extremist views on government and immigration when such views lead to GOP irrelevance?

Some Republicans understand the new demographic map and have tried to get electoral votes awarded by congressional district rather than by state. This smacks of desperation, the panicked response of a party that has diminished its chances of winning the presidency. And by being unable to win the presidency, what guarantee does the GOP have that a Democratic administration won't simply enforce those aspects of immigration reform law that it agrees with? Such is the predicament of a party that has repeatedly committed self-sabotage.

Immigration policy should be based on evidence, not dogma. Supporting amnesty is the right and practical thing to do, but there is no practical political benefit to the GOP in hiking annual immigration levels into the stratosphere.

It's prudent to accept *some* specialists, which is why a skills-based policy that takes in 200,000-400,000 immigrants a year makes more sense than mass immigration. But almost all of America's STEM graduates should be utilized first, and the number of H1-B visas handed out each year should be reduced to 40,000.

And shouldn't American politicians make it a priority to fund job-training programs in towns across America instead of catering to corporate demands to bring in labor from abroad? Shouldn't the input of America's working poor and the middle class be drafted into immigration legislation, not the input of corporate executives?

In not many places in Ohio and Michigan does one see working class folks jumping up and down for joy over the prospect of a greatly increased immigration intake. The middle class isn't doing a jig either. One would think neocons would get the message, and if they weren't such globalist dogmatists, maybe they would.

As with anything, pros and cons should be examined. California, for example, has embraced large numbers of immigrants and the state maintains the innovative and creative dynamism that has helped to define it for a century. It also has substantial income disparities and considerable unemployment, but has moved in the right direction by substantially hiking its minimum wage. California will continue to benefit from specialist immigration, but does a state with more people than Canada really need more mass immigration? If so, why?

And a news flash for the GOP: California has gone from being a state that Richard Nixon and Ronald Reagan could win repeatedly to a state where the GOP is scarcely relevant. *Take the evidence at face value. Don't try to imagine something different.*

Neoconservatives are blind to the negative aspects of mass immigration and especially blind to what it means for the GOP. If many years ago, the GOP had espoused common sense policies of a working class friendly platform and raised taxes on the wealthy, stayed out of pointless wars, protected American jobs, increased the minimum wage, kept legal immigration to under half a million a year, and controlled America's southern border, the GOP wouldn't now be wondering what went wrong in Election 2012. Republicans wouldn't now be facing national political oblivion.

Chapter 4
Society

~~Words~~

Many liberals are committed to a free society, but many others on the left have become intolerant of the most basic aspects of liberty: freedom of expression and speech.

Political correctness didn't appear out of the ether. Speech codes came into being because free speech on campus was thought by some to be a bad thing and those who thought it bad were liberals. Some on the left venerate "diversity" and then bemoan the diversity of opinion essential to a free society.

Whatever faults conservatives have, trying to prevent others from speaking is not one of them, or at least isn't a major one. How often do conservatives demand a TV show be shut down because of its liberal content or insist liberal heads of companies not bring their business to cities for espousing liberal political views? Compare this to the seemingly endless instances of leftists trying to silence those who disagree with them.

Some liberals argue that free speech on campus needs to be opposed to make universities more tolerant, but how is it tolerant to shut people up? The Soviet Union shut people up. Surely, liberals know this. Moreover, many liberals are selective as to what constitutes inappropriate speech and which people they want to shut up. They have no desire to limit extreme-left speech and will ironically invoke "free speech" to defend Marxists.

The definition of a bigot in the view of some liberals is anyone who has an opinion contrary to theirs. If in a multicultural society you need to shut people up for stating their opinions, then what does that say about the nature of a multicultural society? It won't be a place where freedom and individualism will be tolerated for long. And surely those who oppose diversity of opinion and speech must realize that they have zero right to complain if one day someone with power comes along and decides to shut them up.

Benjamin Franklin summed up well the distinction between democracy and liberty: "Democracy is two wolves and a lamb voting on what to have for lunch. Liberty is a well-armed lamb contesting the vote."

In other words, democracy means fifty percent plus one and can result in tyranny, particularly if the population is apathetic, easily led, and more inclined to political fashion, wanting to appear "hip" to the powers that be. Liberty requires a premium be placed on independent thought and speech.

It was Kafkaesque that political correctness should have become entrenched in America at about the same time that communism was falling in Central and Eastern Europe. That something called "political correctness" exists at all indicates cultural dimness.

Conservatives should oppose attempts by those who would replace free speech with fashion statements. Where conservatives get it wrong sometimes is to think that all liberals want to shut them up when a prominent conservative takes a stand opposing gay marriage, for example, and is then criticized. In this case, liberals are also partaking in free speech. There's a difference between criticism and silencing.

A well-functioning society needs open discussion and debate. Policy should be based on the evidence. On some issues, the evidence supports conservative arguments, and for others, the liberal ones. Often, both sides have valid points. And not every issue has to descend into an ideological brawl. Finding common ground is usually a better option.

Narrative

Some on the left have forged a paradigm whereby race and culture have replaced class and economics as primary units and determinants of society. Some peoples are to be lauded, others not, the sole criterion being skin color. Such a schema ignores reality. For much of history, man has been more interested in power, status, and glory than co-existence. When human beings in a stronger position came into contact with human beings in a weaker position, those in the weaker position usually lost out. This has occurred numerous times irrespective of race or national origin.

The British and Spaniards forged empires, oppressing other peoples in the process, but so did the Mongols, Turks, and Japanese. Europeans oppressed other Europeans, Asians other Asians, and Africans other Africans.

Slavery has existed for thousands of years. It still exists in parts of the world today. The word "slave" is derived from "Slav." For centuries, non-European slave raiders ventured into Slavic lands to obtain Slavic slaves, making a mockery of the left's simplistic notion of white oppressors and non-white victims.

In the first millennium AD, Arab and Turkic slavers acquired large numbers of Slavic slaves. In 1241, the Mongols invaded Central and Eastern Europe, and within months, more than a third of Hungary's population perished as the result of slaughter and epidemics. Other parts of Central and Eastern Europe suffered a similar fate. The Mongols conquered Kiev, killed the population, and destroyed the city. They tore through Russia and Poland, destroying towns and killing their inhabitants. For centuries, Tatars launched slave raids against Russia, killing or enslaving millions of Slavs.

The Mongols brought to Europe, Yersinia pestis, the bacterium that causes bubonic plague. In 1347, from their Crimean base in Kaffa, Tatars catapulted plague-ridden corpses at European soldiers, an early form of biological warfare. Within several years, one-third of Europe's population would be dead.

Western Europe also experienced non-European incursion. Spain was invaded by the Moors and endured centuries of occupation. In 732, Charles Martel halted the Muslim advance into Europe at the Battle of Tours. The Ottoman Turks occupied the Balkans for centuries, making their way to the gates of Vienna, where Jan Sobieski and the Poles stopped them in 1683.

From bases in North Africa, the Barbary Pirates captured thousands of English, French, Italian, and Spanish ships, and hundreds of thousands of West European slaves. They seized American ships and

American slaves, and launched slave raids against coastal settlements as far north as England and Ireland, and even Iceland!

Hundreds of thousands of Irish were killed during the Irish Confederate Wars in the mid-17th Century. To put this in context, Ireland's population at the time was 1.5 million. Many Irish were enslaved and sent to Colonial America or the Caribbean, where they often died from maltreatment and disease. In the 19th Century, more than one million Irish starved to death during the Irish Potato Famine and another million fled to the United States. Ireland was England's first colony and a brutalized one. How do the Irish qualify as a privileged people?

Tens of thousands of European Americans died in coalmines to make America a superpower. Many others died from black lung disease. Still others met their end in steel mills and slaughterhouses. Industrial society was cruel and life was short for industrial workers. European Americans dying in the blackness of an American coalmine were not experiencing "white privilege" as they breathed their last. Polish Americans did not enjoy "white privilege" as a sheriff's posse was murdering them during the Lattimer Massacre.

French Acadians were expelled from what is now Maritime Canada. Italian Americans were lynched in several U.S. states in the 19th Century. Polish Americans were drafted disproportionally into the U.S. Army during the world wars. Entry into the middle class for most Slavic Americans only became a reality after the Second World War and it had nothing to do with "white privilege."

Slavs were never "white" in nativist Anglo-American society. They were hewers of wood and drawers of water, useful biological machines to turn America into an industrial superpower, nothing more. Historically, few groups have been as brutalized. More than 50 million Slavs were killed in the 20th Century alone.

In 1837, Missouri governor, Lilburn Boggs, issued his "Mormon Extermination Order," which resulted in expulsion of Missouri's Mormons to Illinois. Nativists viewed Roman Catholics with hostility until recently and anti-Catholicism isn't considered gauche in some liberal circles.

Numerous ethnic and religious groups have experienced oppression in the United States. The poor of all nationalities suffered more than others. There is no ethnic group with a presence in the United States of more than a century, including English Americans, whose members did not at one time experience privation in America.

While it's important to remember past oppression, it's inappropriate to put ethnic or racial groups into "privileged" or "oppressed" categories. Not only is it historically misleading (the privileged were usually the upper classes, who made up a sliver of Britain's population, for example) but it also leads to division and polarization.

A homeless man of British descent in an American city is not privileged, and it's more than likely his 18th or 19th Century ancestors weren't privileged either. Most likely they spent long days toiling away at manual and often dangerous labor.

In this century, America's class divide, the widening gap between rich and poor, encompasses all races, and politicians and policy makers should focus their attention on shoring up the middle class and helping the poor of all backgrounds.

Affirmative Action

Conservatives should work to expand opportunity for all Americans. Inclusive affirmative action is one step in that direction, and it would give conservatives the moral high ground over exclusionary liberal policies.

A case can be made for some forms of affirmative action, for the disabled and for the poor, for example, and the program should be dealt with holistically. Conservatives are right to oppose any affirmative policy that uses race as a criterion, but excludes ethnic origin.

There is no justification, historical or otherwise, to exclude Americans of Slavic, Irish, Hungarian, and Italian descent from affirmative action policies. Nor should affirmative action be denied to introverts, gay men, transgendered persons, older persons, and poor Anglo-Americans.

White ethnics and working class whites are underrepresented at many elite universities, and government should encourage universities to create inclusive student bodies. Military academies should extend affirmative action to white ethnics and corporations should prioritize white ethnics in hiring and promotion.

From an ethical standpoint, how can the Republican Party say no to affirmative action for Irish, Polish, and Italian Americans, while not demanding an end to it for other ethnic or racial groups? Republicans should call for affirmative action to be expanded to include white ethnics, or otherwise demand the end of a race-based version of the policy. The GOP won't be able to avoid the issue if amnesty goes through, so they might as well address it and get it out of the way.

Like the minimum wage, affirmative action is an easy issue for the GOP to take off the table. Call for the end of a version that includes race but not ethnic origin, using economic criteria instead, or embrace an inclusive race and ethnic version with an economic aspect as part of it. In other words, keep it for existing groups, but expand it to include other groups.

Extroversion is seen as the norm in American society. In a country biased toward extroversion, personality type should be a basis for affirmative action.

Gay white men and white transgendered individuals continue to suffer from bigotry. Many gay white men live in larger cities, having moved there from smaller towns. Upon arrival, they find themselves a minority twice over: being white and being gay. This sometimes makes them a target of racial and homophobic violence, the two hatreds often wrapped up as one. Affirmative action needs to be extended to gay white men and white transgendered individuals.

Given the pervasiveness of institutional liberal racism, affirmative action should be extended to poor Americans of English, Scottish, and Scots-Irish origin.

Many on the racist left look down on Appalachian WASPs as inbred hicks who mate with their cousins in trailer parks and pop oxycontins like popcorn. Open the doors of the Ivy League and Fortune 500 to the sons and daughters of Appalachia.

Workers over 40 have a hard time in the job market. Ageism is unacceptable and companies should use goals and timetables to ensure older folks get hired.

Relatively few conservatives are employed as professors in the humanities and social sciences, and conservative journalists aren't welcome in most American media. A person's life views should be considered a basis for affirmative action. Diversity of opinion in academia and media makes society more inclusive.

Making sure a Slavic American has a fair shot at getting into an Ivy League school or of becoming an executive in a Fortune 500 company isn't going to collapse the Good Ole Boys' Club. Making a gay man a Marine general isn't going to emasculate the military.

Diversity in the workplace is laudable, but it should be an inclusive diversity, not diversity based on the illusion of inclusion. By adopting inclusive policies, conservatives show they care about ordinary people.

Gay Marriage

Some conservatives believe homosexuality a sin. Well, gluttony, sloth, and greed are deadly sins, and plenty of obese, lazy, and greedy folks get married, and in church no less.

Divorced folks are allowed to remarry. Why don't social conservatives obsess about divorce? Or is it acceptable for social conservatives to indulge in the cultural relativism they supposedly decry? Divorced straight people should be the last folks to oppose gay marriage unless they take the hypocritical stance that only straight people should be permitted social liberalism.

The reason gay marriage has been so quickly accepted in America is that those who oppose it have no rational basis for their opposition. Now if divorce were banned in America...oh wait, many of the same social conservatives opposed to gay marriage would scream bloody murder, claiming their rights were being infringed upon.

What about outlawing premarital heterosexual sex? If social conservatives want social conservatism, they should be prepared to accept it for themselves, shouldn't they? For that matter, all forms of sex that don't lead to procreation should be banned, including oral sex. This writer can just see social conservative jaws dropping. "No, no," the response would be, "social liberalism is okay for us. It's only the gays who can't have it. After all, we're good ole boys." <Writer rolls eyes>

America isn't in the business of allowing religion to dictate who can and cannot get married. Marriage isn't exclusively partnered with religion. Atheists and agnostics get married all the time, at city hall or a county office. Should atheists and agnostics be prohibited from get married?

Gays don't procreate is an argument used by gay marriage foes. Well, a lot of straights choose not to procreate and some can't. Should they be prevented from getting married? Should it be illegal for older heterosexuals to get married?

In many Western countries, fertility rates are below replacement level. Should heterosexuals who want one child be prohibited from getting married? One child per couple over many generations amounts to evolutionary failure. Why don't social conservatives decry one-child parents as evolutionary failures and demand their marriages be annulled?

Another argument against gay marriage is that it opens the door to adoption by gay parents. But it's not easy to adopt kids, nor should it be. A gay couple meeting the requirements associated with adoption could surely provide a decent life for a child.

Social conservatives sometimes make a political calculations argument that supporting gay marriage results in conservatives staying at home on Election Day. But conservative voters already stay home, despite opposition to same-sex marriage by Republican presidential candidates. One would think it would make the GOP reexamine things.

Polls show the public increasingly supportive of gay marriage. The white working class is split down the middle on the issue with most young working class voters in favor. Supporting same-sex marriage doesn't hurt conservatives in a presidential election and might even help them in swing states. It's also consistent with the live-and-let-live underpinning of American conservatism. Conservatives should make sensible choices to get socially moderate voters on their side. Supporting gay marriage is one way to do it.

Abortion

Just as in an ideal world there would be no affirmative action, in an ideal world there would be no abortion. Every embryo would be allowed to develop into a human being.

But in the real world, abortion policy should take into account basic questions: If a woman gives birth to a child and has no capacity to look after it, who is to pay for the baby? Who will feed the child, clothe it, and send it to school for two decades?

These questions speak to the hypocrisy of some conservatives. They speak of less government and of cutting welfare and food stamps, but expect an impoverished mother to look after a child she can't possibly look after. It's not a logical position to hold. One can't have it both ways and be rational. One can't say no to abortion and then demand cuts to social programs.

It's easy for a man to take an anti-abortion stance because he can never know what it's like to be in the position of a woman struggling to decide whether or to not give birth to an unborn child.

Conservatives have to look at this issue as if they were standing in another person's shoes. By all means, advocate counseling and social help, including welfare and housing if the woman decides to keep the child, but the decision should remain hers.

Abortion has been a highly charged and divisive issue for decades. Unlike gay rights, where the social pendulum has swung to an anti-discriminatory position, polls on abortion have held steady. People dislike abortion, but neither do they want to outlaw it completely.

Roe vs. Wade won't be overturned. Conservatives should focus instead on creating conditions that lead to fewer abortions.

Gun Control

Gun murder in America is at a multi-decade low. Many attribute this decline to mandatory sentencing laws and longer jail terms that have led to a tripling of the prison population since the late 1980s. Some point to proactive and predictive policing. Others point to the fall in the birth rate and an aging population, as young men constitute a smaller percentage of the population today than 30 years ago. Some credit the decline in gun murder to gentrification of inner cities and surveillance technologies.

There are some 300 million privately owned guns in America, although the percentage of Americans owning guns has fallen over the last 30 years. Guns are easy to purchase in many states and some of America's safest neighborhoods have a high percentage of gun owners. In white neighborhoods, violent crime, including gun murder, is rare. Barring calamity or a substantial growth in gang membership, gun violence should continue to decline. It's hard to envisage gun crime rising in an aging America.

An assault weapons ban is reasonable and should be supported, but it's a decision that should be left to the states. It would be arrogant to foist the laws of New York or Illinois on Montana and North Dakota, as it would be arrogant to do the reverse.

Gun enthusiasts, and there are many in America, like to spend time at firing ranges. Most gun enthusiasts are responsible, law-abiding citizens. Many have served in the military. States that outlaw assault weapons can strike a balance by allowing citizens to go to firing ranges where they can rent assault rifles, blasting away to their heart's content. Weapons are then returned and locked away.

Second, stiff sentences should be meted out for gun crimes. Third, proactive policing is an important part of any gun crime reduction strategy, which means a strong police presence in neighborhoods with serious gun violence. This does not mean stop-and-frisk as such a policy can reasonably be seen as a violation of the Fourth Amendment. To search ordinary people going about their business is dubious at best and Marxist at worst. It's an invasion of privacy and an assault on dignity. Many violent criminals are repeat offenders known to police, and arresting individuals who reoffend should be done with minimal inconvenience to the general population.

Mass shootings are rare, but steps can be taken to make them even less frequent. In many such cases, the shooter suffers from mental illness. Firearms should be denied to persons taking multiple psychotropic drugs and to individuals who have been diagnosed with serious mental illness. Psychological evaluations should be considered for people wanting to purchase assault weapons.

Prospective gun owners should undergo background checks and be required to take a firearms course, completion of which leads to a firearms license. Guns should be registered and liability insurance should be a requirement of gun ownership.

To some extent, America has become a narcissistic country where making it big on reality TV, getting a million views on the Internet, or having a thousand online "friends" has become the be-all and end-all for some people. Video games glorify killing. The more virtual people a gamer kills, and in the most grotesque ways possible, the more points the person wins. For some people, society has become a simulation, a hyper-reality fame game. For a few mentally ill narcissists, becoming a mass killer is the ultimate form of attention whoring.

Mass shootings will remain infrequent because few people are so mentally ill or malevolent enough to commit them. Conservatives need to play a proactive role in formulating a gun crime reduction strategy that takes into account all elements leading to gun violence.

Chapter 5
Economy

Limits of Laissez Faire — Healthcare

The market is always right. It's a common neocon view that's easily proven false. In parts of the world, body parts of endangered animals are purchased for various reasons. If the market were always right, it would be okay to hunt the Siberian Tiger and Snow Leopard to extinction.

America's healthcare system consumes about 17.5 percent of America's GDP. Other developed countries, using some variation of an individual mandate or single payer health scheme, spend 10-13 percent of GDP on medical care. Medical tests like MRIs are less expensive in these countries. Life spans are longer. How is the market always right when applied to medical care?

American medical specialists often charge more for treatment than specialists in other countries. Some specialists own or are investors in labs or surgery centers where tests and procedures are done, and billing is designed to maximize a doctor's profit. How is the market right for patients?

If Obamacare is an unsalvageable disaster, Republicans have an opportunity to win the White House in 2016, but GOP victory would not be a sure thing. The 2016 Democratic presidential candidate would likely campaign for a single payer system in response to an Obamacare fiasco. Any GOP alternative to Obamacare that panders to the rich could result in

Democrats winning the White House in 2016 even if Obamacare leads to higher premiums for millions.

Why could the Democratic candidate still win? Because Obamacare is not state-run medical care. It's a private sector approach to making private medical coverage fairer. If such an approach fails, Democrats could say that the real problem is laissez faire and then call for single payer healthcare. The GOP might not win that argument. Why? *Because the market is sometimes wrong.*

It's almost as if a chess game is being played with healthcare. The private health system is broken, so along comes Obamacare. Republicans call it a disaster and some Democrats come to the same realization. Speculatively, the 2016 Republican presidential candidate unveils a medical plan, which in true GOP style benefits the wealthy. Republicans can't help themselves and Democrats know this. The Democrats counter by advocating single payer, which some will say was the Democrats' plan all along. Voters, reeling from rising healthcare premiums, elect a Democratic president on the promise of single payer. Checkmate.

<In an alternative parallel universe, or in and odd version of this one, Republicans win 43 states in the 2016 presidential election and this writer is busy writing a book, When Donkeys Croak: A Somewhat Satirical Take On Democrat Demise>

Restoring Tax Fairness

Low taxes for the rich and trickle-down economics are neocon commandments. But tax cuts in the 2000s in concert with a deregulated Wall Street and globalization led to the most serious economic downturn in America since the Great Depression.

By contrast, economic growth was higher and living standards rose substantially under Republican President, Dwight Eisenhower, when the top marginal tax rate was 90 percent. Eisenhower showed that progressive tax policies are consistent with American conservatism.

The upper middle class needs to pay more to help eliminate the deficit, bring down the debt, and keep government programs intact. This means a tax rate of 40 percent on individual income above $80,000, and on family income above $140,000.

Conservatives should support a tax rate of 47 percent on individual income above $140,000, and on family income above $200,000. The rate should rise to 60 percent on individual or family income above $300,000.

Singles making less than $25,000 should be exempt from paying income tax, as should families making less than $35,000. The first $25,000 a single man makes is shelter money, food money. It's survival money and it would be wrong to tax it. If the math doesn't add up revenue-wise, adjustments can be made at higher income levels, and/or by using means other than income tax to make up the difference (i.e. by transferring social program costs to corporations by increasing the minimum wage – see Chapter 3).

In the spirit of social justice, a 1 percent wealth tax should be levied on folks with a net worth of more than $50 million, rising to 3 percent on a net worth of more than $200 million. This will help bring fairness to a country that for too long has pampered the rich.

Capital gains should be taxed at a rate of 40 percent once an individual has made more than $10 million in the casino.

Spending Cuts

Cutting spending is part of the debt-fighting equation, but a large part of the debt can be blamed on anemic economic growth, and medical costs of an inefficient healthcare system. Growing the economy at more than 3 percent annually, which has been normal after recessions, would help reduce the deficit and eventually the debt.

Bringing healthcare spending down from 17.5 percent of GDP to 12-13 percent would save hundreds of billions a year. If the Affordable Care Act doesn't reduce costs enough, healthcare should be nationalized. Conservatives should want to save money on healthcare while offering quality medical care to the working and middle classes. A single payer system is conservative medical care, as it lowers costs, cuts bureaucracy, and puts patient interests ahead of interests of drug and insurance companies.

Increased medical spending on an aging population will be partially offset over the next 40 years by sophisticated methods of detecting and treating disease, resulting in shorter hospital stays and lower treatment costs, despite increases in drug prices. People will live longer and in a healthier state. By century's end, large hospitals will be shut down because they will no longer be necessary.

A substantial reduction in defense spending is possible if America adopts a realist foreign policy, not a relationship with the world based on endless war. Closing overseas bases, cutting back on waste, and scaling back or cancelling some weapons programs can reduce annual defense spending by $50 billion.

Bringing government salaries down to private sector levels would save billions. Slashing government bureaucracy by 15 percent would yield additional savings. Ironically, the weakening of the middle class has made government jobs all the more sought after and government workers vote for the Democratic Party. The GOP keeps finding ways to grow the Democratic Party's base.

Cutting foreign aid from $50 billion to $30 billion per year makes sense. Foreign aid to help poor countries is appropriate as it generates goodwill for America. It also benefits America to provide military aid to her allies, but foreign aid should be reduced in tough economic times.

Eliminating government waste and downsizing government departments can generate annual savings of $50 billion. Education costs, for example, will decline due to technological innovation. The proliferation of massive open online courses (MOOCs) is part of a trend toward increased virtualization of schooling. Traditional education has left a generation of students saddled with debt, making alternative forms of learning necessary.

And who needs a legion of foreign policy wonks at the State Department when algorithms can take into account all scenarios in any country and the likelihood of their occurring? Savings accrued from dealing successfully with pre-crisis situations will lead to lower defense costs. Algorithmic processes will lead to savings across government departments. Government will become more efficient.

Tariffs, not Free Trade

Neoconservatives support free trade even though it's been disastrous for America. Protectionism has led country after country to economic stardom. The mercantilist British Empire, protectionist America, Bismarck's Germany, Meiji Japan, post-war Japan, and modern-day China and South Korea, have all been examples of this. What country has become great because it practiced free trade?

Globalization has led to stagnant American wages when adjusted for inflation. It's led to record trade deficits. It's resulted in offshoring, bringing misery to millions of American workers.

Manufacturing, which accounted for 28 percent of America's GDP in the 1950s, is now barely 11 percent, even with some reshoring. By contrast, manufacturing accounts for a quarter of Germany's GDP, and Germany exports to the world as much as America, a country with four times Germany's population. America runs budget deficits while Germany, a country experiencing natural population decrease, runs budget surpluses.

Germans are not more able than Americans, but Germany has kept its industrial base intact. No country could match the industrial output of the United States when America pursued its national interest, as occurred in the Second World War. In more recent years, America has been conducting economic self-sabotage, working against its national interest in order to placate corporate greed.

George Washington, Alexander Hamilton, Abraham Lincoln, and Theodore Roosevelt all regarded free trade as quackery. Ronald Reagan not only raised taxes when he had to, but he also limited imports of cars, textiles, and steel to protect the national interest.

Karl Marx supported free trade because he considered it a quick way to destroy nations and capitalism. Why on earth is America happily following the Marxist path to capitalist ruination?

Free trade advocates should consider these questions: Why support free trade when it's led to trillions of dollars in American trade deficits over the last thirty years? Why think it acceptable to offshore millions of American jobs? Why support free trade with China when China puts high tariffs on American goods, making it difficult to sell American products in China? Why should China then be allowed to flood the American marketplace with its goods? The argument that U.S. consumers benefit from cheap Chinese goods doesn't wash, as Americans could afford to buy TVs, refrigerators, and other goods in the 1970s and 1980s. Americans were still being paid decently back then, before so many jobs...were shipped to China...

Free trade, and massive American trade deficits helped make possible the Great Recession, as countries that ran huge trade surpluses with America channeled that wealth into American toxic securities. American workers stripped of decent-paying manufacturing jobs pay less in payroll taxes and this has made funding for Social Security problematic. Free trade has resulted in one negative after another negative for the American people and U.S economy. Why, then, support free trade when it not only doesn't benefit the national interest, but leads to national disaster?

What, then, accounts for neoconservative obsession with the economics of national destruction? Greed is a part of it. Whereas free trade has savaged Main Street, it's benefited corporate bottom lines, lining the pockets of American executives.

Politicians of both parties know that when their congressional careers are over, the real money lies in lobbying. It might never occur to any congressman to make a good impression on a potential future employer. Or maybe it would.

Neocons also have a mindless penchant for universalism. They support free trade in the name of an ideological imperative, out of fealty to dogma, as they recklessly support mass immigration.

Some pundits offer an intriguing defense of free trade: Free trade has helped to keep the world peaceful by channeling energies of major countries into commerce and not war. Hundreds of millions have been lifted out of poverty because of free trade, so the argument goes, and this has made the world more peaceful and secure. This argument offers a pessimistic view of the world and human nature and basically states that in the absence of free trade, war is likely and perhaps inevitable.

If this view is correct, then America should continue with free trade even though it has weakened the United States economically, but there is no evidence to support the premise. In the absence of globalization and free trade, America avoided getting into a war with the Soviet Union and China during the Cold War. The argument also implies that, but for America having allowed itself to become a dumping ground for foreign products, other countries would have been unable to modernize, which is hardly a rational perspective.

Conservatives should support tariffs and other policies to make America the world's preeminent center of high-end manufacturing. The tax rate on American companies that manufacture their products in the United States should fall to 10 percent. American companies that maintain primary manufacturing operations abroad should be taxed at 60 percent.

China's trade surplus with America is larger than its total trade surplus with the world. A tariff of 15-20 percent on Chinese goods would not be too onerous on China as it transitions from an export-driven economy to an economy based on exports, internal consumption, and innovation. The American-China trade relationship should be a balanced one, not skewed heavily in China's favor.

China's access to the world's natural and technological resources will increase in coming decades because China's government will help Chinese industry acquire these things. Beijing is targeting and buying cutting-edge Western companies to boost Chinese knowhow so that China can become a manufacturer of high-end goods and world technology leader.

The PRC's economic and military strength will increase substantially through China's own efforts, but also because America will likely remain beholden to an open-markets-at-all-costs philosophy. China is not the economic threat to America some imagine it to be, but that could change in 20 years, particularly if America continues with self-destructive policies.

It would not be surprising for China in the 2030s to be producing world-class automobiles, appliances, and electronics, with American industry trailing behind. Who knows, perhaps bankrupt Detroit, or other parts of Michigan, or New York, will become North American centers of Chinese industry with Americans working for the Chinese. The reader might say "impossible," but Mao's ghost might get the last laugh. America's Founders, by contrast, are already spinning in their graves.

Toward a Mixed Economy

Collaboration between government and industry hastens technological progress and economic development. For those who doubt this, ask two questions: Did the Manhattan and Apollo programs hurt or benefit America? Would America have been better off had it left development of the atom bomb to private industry during the Second World War?

Competition in an open marketplace leads to innovation, too, and this has served America in the past, but some things are too important to be left solely to the private sector. America should move toward a two-tier economic model of free enterprise and state capitalism. Aside from the usual regulations of running a company, most businesses should function free of government interference. The vast majority of American companies should continue to operate under a free enterprise paradigm.

By contrast, government should support Critical Core Industries. Much of the auto industry was in such dire straits that government had to rescue it, but the auto industry should not have been allowed to become so dilapidated that it needed rescuing in the first place.

Abraham Lincoln helped to lay down the steel and railroads foundation of the modern American state. Lincoln loathed free trade. America today needs a Lincoln to dragoon a moribund economy away from the backwardness of free trade and globalism to the economic optimization made possible by a synergy of free enterprise, state capitalism, and tariffs.

Government oversight committees should be ensconced in areas critical to the national interest. This should be done in the context of an American industrial strategy whereby government and the private sector partner to advance vital technologies and industries.

Partnership would involve these areas: automobiles, programmable matter technology, nanotechnology, biotech engineering and genomics, pharmaceutical development, artificial intelligence and robotics, advanced propulsion technologies, space exploration technologies, quantum and biological/organic computer technologies, environmental and renewable energy technologies, new energy technologies, advanced defense technologies, cyber warfare systems, information technologies, neural interface technologies, manufacturing and materials technologies, 3D manufacturing technologies, teleportation technologies, light manipulation and holographic technologies, educational technologies, food production and agriculture technologies, telescopic technologies, mining and resource extraction technologies.

The Chinese keep their most advanced technologies under wraps. By contrast, some American companies transfer part of their R&D to China, employing Chinese scientists and engineers. America's transfer of R&D to China has been a good thing for China, but America's technological lead over the PRC has dwindled in a way few could have imagined 30 years ago.

A Department of Science and Industry should be established to sync government R&D and money with industry and private capital to develop and commercialize new products. DSI would facilitate America's reindustrialization with high-end manufacturing, as well as hastening technological development. Any company wishing to do business with DSI would be required to keep its primary manufacturing operations, and all of its R&D, in the United States.

Making Workers Corporate Partners

Corporations should value their workers. American companies should adopt something similar to the German model of codetermination. It is a system where worker representatives are included in the supervisory board of directors of German companies.

American workers should have a say as to whether they want their jobs offshored. What neocons never understood is that corporations need not choose between people and profits. As Germany has demonstrated, a win-win situation is possible: profitable companies, padding their bottom lines, based at home, benefiting native workers and the nation.

Germany is not a perfect model for America in so far as underemployment is rife in Germany as it is in the United States. The point is America can and should emulate positive aspects of other countries' economic models and Americanize them.

Rein in Finance Capitalism

Investment banking and private equity management companies should be taxed at a rate of 60 percent to take into account the moral hazard posed by them to the U.S. economy. Financial services companies that try to avoid paying American taxes by setting up overseas tax arrangements should be heavily fined.

Wall Street requires extensive regulation. Conservatives should demand big banks be nationalized and broken up. If something is too big to fail, it's too big. It's odd that people who call themselves conservatives, and who rail against big government, should then turn around and applaud like trained seals, big banks.

After being divided up into manageable entities, investment banks can again operate as private firms, but should be required to write checks, equal to a third of their profits, to be divided up and paid to working and middle class citizens. The cost of administrating this would be borne by the banks.

Sharing Natural Resource Wealth

Oil and gas profits should be taxed at a rate of 50-60 percent. This is the people's wealth. With America's energy reserves surpassing Saudi Arabia's, some energy profits should each year be placed into an energy trust fund to help keep Social Security solvent. Natural resource checks should also be given to working and middle class Americans on an annual basis.

Toward a Guaranteed Basic Income

As robots and AI lead to productivity gains and worker displacement, calls for a Guaranteed Basic Income will grow. Social spending could fall if the government gave an annual $10,000 check to every American, to be indexed to inflation and increased proportionately to future productivity gains. A basic financial safety net would also reduce stress, which would lead to medical cost savings. A Guaranteed Basic Income would be affordable, too, if America started to run substantial budget surpluses. While a Guaranteed Basic Income won't become a reality in this decade, it's almost certain to happen before mid-century. Conservatives would be wise to start making the case for it now.

Conclusion

The national debt can be reduced, and decent economic growth attained, if taxes are raised, spending cuts are implemented, healthcare is nationalized, tariffs are placed on most foreign products, American industry is partnered with government, Wall Street is regulated, investment banks are broken up, America's energy bonanza is managed properly, and crises that lead to higher interest rates are averted.

Chapter 6
IDEAS

Conservatives need the "vision thing." People need to dream and so do countries. Government put man in space and made a trip to the moon possible. What dream better to fire imaginations than a faster-than-light capability that would allow man to explore the galaxy? Recent advances hold out the possibility that such technology might not be as far-fetched as previously thought.

Conservatives should champion research into space propulsion technologies to end man's reliance on chemical rockets. Costs would be modest and might one day lead to interstellar flight.

Fusion power, too, seems increasingly possible. Nuclear fusion plants could begin providing clean and safe energy for America by mid-century, eliminating the need for fossil fuels before the century is out. Conservatives should support government involvement in nuclear fusion research, as well as the speedy commercialization of cheap solar panels.

Conservatives should make nanotechnology research a priority. Creating almost any object from raw material could end poverty. Nanomachines might one day be able to cure disease, repair human organs, and eliminate pollution.

3D printers could have a transformative effect on society over the next several decades. Personal manufacturing might bring down costs of everything from clothing to medicines. Widespread use of this technology might accelerate innovation, making ordinary people inventors.

E-Sheets equipped with virtual teacher apps will become ubiquitous to a child's education. Virtual teachers will adapt quickly to the way students learn instead of students having to adjust to the way human teachers teach.

Education spending will fall and students could finish high school and university more quickly than today. Advanced simulation technology will allow students to complete practicums. No books, no attending an institution, no tens of thousands of dollars in debt. In addition to learning the general curriculum, students could focus on subjects that interest them and for which few human teachers are available.

Stress would be reduced in a virtual learning setting, which could yield medical cost savings down the line. Children would feel more confident that they've mastered material. Virtual teachers and personalized education would particularly benefit introverts, who often feel alienated and marginalized by an education system that does little to cater to introvert needs.

Advances in diagnostic technology will mean blood, urine, and breath tests will soon be able to detect most early stage cancers. Medical imaging is improving. By 2050, almost all forms of cancer will be curable or manageable. Conservatives should support an annual increase of ten billion dollars for cancer research to conquer the disease as swiftly as possible.

Conservatives should back development of a green economy. America's decrepit infrastructure requires fixing. Government and the private sector can partner to fund job training and create millions of green and infrastructure jobs.

Finally, and most importantly, get the chant right. It's "trickle-up." It's really that simple and that's the beauty of it. Start with people and not Wall Street. That's the way to rebrand the GOP.

By putting ideas on the table that can benefit the country as a whole, not just the wealthiest segment of it, conservatives can become relevant again.

Chapter 7
Foreign Policy

Irrational Foreign Policy

Neoconservative globalism has few roots in U.S. history. Manifest Destiny and the Monroe Doctrine involved the Americas. The Philippine-American War, which had proto-neoconservative aspects, was an extension of the Spanish-American War, which involved Cuba.

Some neoconservatives invoke Woodrow Wilson, and it's true that some of Wilson's interventions were of a dubious nature, but he did try to steer America clear of major conflicts. Wilson proclaimed neutrality during the First World War and kept America out of the war even after the sinking of the Lusitania, with 120 American civilian dead, and even when it seemed Germany might win. For a time after the Lusitania attack, Germany reduced its attacks on merchant shipping and Wilson kept American troops out of Europe.

Resumption of unrestricted submarine warfare and interception of a telegram from German Foreign Minister, Arthur Zimmerman, to the German ambassador to Mexico, forced Wilson to act. The telegram promised German support to Mexico in acquiring Texas, Arizona, and New Mexico. American public opinion all but forced Wilson's hand, and when he went before Congress, only six senators and 50 congressmen voted against war.

Wilson held out about as long as any American president could under such circumstances. American ships were being attacked and sunk by a country that had the potential to dominate Europe. Zimmerman's telegram indicated that Germany supported carving up the United States. Wilson was an idealist, but his measured approach to war in Europe is seen today as an example of sensible foreign policy.

Reasons for War

Demographic trends might make war less likely. The world's population is aging. Many nations will get old before they get rich, but this should be placed in context: most people in the world live better than their grandparents and this trend will continue.

Materially comfortable, older societies, do not, in general, start wars, but this does not mean war will be relegated to history books. Cultural factors matter. Saving face is important in many cultures. On a crowded planet with finite resources, the need for food, water, and energy could lead to conflict. Some governments might choose war to deflect from domestic failings. As robots become more fully integrated into the world's armies, proxy machine wars might replace conventional combat with robots and drones battling it out instead of people.

Countries threatened by other states might lash out on the theory that the best defense is a good offense. Imperialism remains a reason for war. Dictatorships are by their nature unpredictable and might resort to war for many reasons. Ideology matters. America started a war against Iraq out of neocon ideological zeal so fanatical that all intelligence contrary to what the American government wanted to hear was ignored.

Technological dispersal has helped to modernize societies. In countries where landline telephones were never common, cellular networks have allowed these societies to leapfrog over a technology ubiquitous to the developed world for a century. There was no need to reinvent the wheel.

Similarly, quality education will spread rapidly to the poorest regions of the Earth as cheap e-Sheets running sophisticated teaching apps will allow students to learn almost anything. Developing countries won't need to build an expensive bricks and mortar education system. Why construct Ivy League quality universities when almost any subject can be taught to someone living anywhere in the world with a cheap piece of digital paper that can be folded and pocketed?

What does this have to do with foreign policy? A better-off, better-educated world is one where nationalism is becoming stronger. Internationalism for its own sake is largely a Western ideology; it barely exists in the non-Western world. Blowback will become more severe if America continues to meddle recklessly in other countries' affairs.

Barring development of sentient and malevolent machines, nuclear weapons and MAD will contain robot wars, as they prevented a clash between the United States and the Soviet Union during the Cold War.

Realism in Europe

A realist foreign policy is the most rational way to engage a nationalist world. This does not mean isolationism, but realpolitik. America's close ties with its NATO allies, and with Japan, South Korea, Australia, New Zealand, and Israel, should be kept in place.

Realism exists in Russian-American relations. The tacit agreement between Russia and America is that territory of the former Soviet Union minus the Baltic States will remain within the Russian military sphere of influence. NATO will not expand eastward. In return, Russia won't interfere in Central European states belonging to the Western cultural sphere.

British foreign policy has historically been based on the idea that no European nation should be allowed to become a continental hegemon. America has emulated this approach and should continue to do so.

NATO's purpose must be to ensure European territorial integrity and security, not fighting wars on other continents. To this end, America should provide military aid to Poland, which has been a strong American ally, and to other former Warsaw Pact states. This will strengthen NATO's eastern perimeter.

Human rights in Russia are important, but the American government and media should stop picking and choosing which countries' human right records to condemn. America should criticize Russia's treatment of gays, but to not then make stronger protests against countries that treat gays far worse than Russia is so much hypocrisy. The United States needs to show consistency on gay rights, not selective outrage.

The EU should expand. If the EU still exists in 2035, Ukraine, Serbia, and possibly Turkey could be a part of it. Ukraine and Serbia should not be shut out of Europe's most important club.

The EU poses no threat to Russia, nor would a prosperous Ukraine. By contrast, a stagnant Ukraine could lead to instability in that country, which would not benefit Russia, and a corrupt Ukraine subservient to Russia would ensure Ukrainian stagnation.

Ukrainians want good relations with both Russia and the EU and it's not the EU that insists Ukraine choose one side or the other, and if it chooses the wrong side, then hostile measures might be imposed on the country. Ukrainians have the right to a decent economic future and not have their sovereignty impinged upon.

EU expansion will benefit poorer European countries and German manufacturers will continue to profit by using the Euro, which keeps German exports cheap relative to a reintroduced Deutsche Mark. An influx of young European immigrants will assimilate into German society. Robots will augment Germany's workforce, but given Germany's aging population this will initially be a positive development. Keeping Germany and France prosperous and stable will help to ensure European security and order.

Collapse of the Euro Zone, either in whole or in part, would lead to reassessment of the European project, but it would not lead to a continent-wide slide into national chauvinism. Core EU nations are too interconnected economically and have worked too hard ending old antagonisms to allow history to become farce.

The EU and NATO have allowed European nations to replace rivalry, mistrust, and conflict with economic and security cooperation. Conservatives should continue to support European economic and military integration.

Rational Foreign Policy in the Middle East

Rational American foreign policy in the Islamic world means not starting wars there. Iran hasn't invaded anyone since the 1979 Islamic revolution and its economy has been stricken by sanctions. It almost had a Persian Spring, which might yet occur. Despite 20 years of neocon agitation over Iran's civilian nuclear program, Iran still does not have a deliverable nuclear weapon, let alone a nuclear arsenal.

Conservatives should work for a permanent deal with Iran that allows for inspections of Iranian nuclear facilities and an ending of any Iranian military nuclear ambitions in exchange for sanctions against Iran being lifted and a normal economic relationship between Iran and America being forged. This is doable as Iranians are tired of having a strained relationship with the United States.

Conservatives should continue to support Israel, and they should also support creation of a Palestinian state. A prerequisite for justice and a lasting peace in the Middle East is a viable Palestine, which will also contribute to Israel's security. A one-state solution would be unlikely, as the majority of Israelis would oppose it.

Unless a Palestinian state is established, eventually, inevitably, that unresolved issue is going to explode. If

Israel continues with an untenable status quo, the Palestinians will eventually revolt. The way out is to establish a territorially contiguous Palestinian state.

Conservatives need to be honest brokers in the Middle East, maintaining strong friendship with Israel and showing that friendship by opposing boycotts of Israel (hypocritical at the very least) and by being committed to the defense of Israel, but conservatives should also be honest with Israeli leaders by indicating displeasure at a stalled peace process and Israel's continued expansion of West Bank settlements.

Terrorism

In so far as there are autonomous terrorist groups in chaotic places, these groups can be monitored. If any attack, or on the verge of attacking, the United States, they can be taken out in a counter-terror operation, using drones, air strikes and/or Special Forces, not an invasion of another country.

Sino-American Relations

China is an American economic rival, but there is little to indicate that this rivalry will lead to military conflict. China holds too much American debt and China's trade surplus is so skewed toward America that Beijing is unlikely to risk war with the United States.

China has arguably benefited from globalization more than any other country. Over the last 35 years, China has invested and exported its way to prosperity, carefully nurturing its own industries even as Washington threw American manufacturing under the bus.

But China's success has led to rising expectations of its people and Beijing fears social upheaval. According to some estimates, the PRC faces thousands of strikes, industrial actions, and civil disturbances each year.

The years of 10 percent economic growth are likely over for China and Beijing has shown itself cautious and pragmatic on the world stage, using commerce, not military force, to advance Chinese power. It's unlikely China will make a claim to world leadership anytime soon. The current world order suits China. Unless China undergoes a bout of madness, tensions between China and America will remain confined to the economic sphere. U.S. conservatives should push for deals with China that address concerns of currency manipulation, intellectual theft, and unfair trade practices.

One caveat to a peaceful American-Chinese future lies in Chinese cyber warfare capabilities. Any Chinese war against the United States would begin with massive cyber attacks on American critical systems.

American quiescence over Chinese cyber attacks not only emboldens China, but the Chinese become more proficient in circumventing American computer defenses with each new attack. In event of war, America might not have the benefit of a cyber strike playbook to fall back on. China would. America could be at a disadvantage in the face of a coordinated Chinese cyber, conventional, and asymmetric assault on the United States, which might include hypersonic weapons and an EMP attack. In such a scenario, the United States could face collapse.

China's cyber warfare, spying, and asymmetric capabilities might develop to the point where Beijing might conclude military victory over America probable. America's tepid response to Chinese cyber attacks might make conflict more likely.

That America has spent trillions on unnecessary wars, but has done little to protect itself from an EMP attack is unfathomable. America's critical systems infrastructure should be upgraded to make it resistant to an electromagnetic pulse.

America can't keep ignoring China's theft of U.S. intellectual property, for it amounts to tens of billions of dollars each year and makes the United States look inept. So long as China can steal American technology at will, and so long as America does little in response, what incentive would Chinese negotiators have to sit at a table with American envoys, discuss ending cyber espionage, and do anything other than yawn?

It's senseless for America to spend hundreds of billions on the F-35, only to have China take the blueprints with the ease of someone picking up a leaf from the ground. It's as if the U.S. government has accepted that China will steal American technology as part of the price of doing business with the PRC, even when that price already entails America running massive annual trade deficits with China. Bizarre undeniably, but the gods of globalization must be satisfied.

Conservatives should push for a comprehensive treaty with Beijing that ends cyber warfare and espionage between America and China. A tit-for-tat scenario of hacking and hacking back should be avoided. Many computers used for hacking don't belong to the hackers and innocent people could be harmed. Moreover, a hacking conflict could escalate into a conventional military one.

The world of the first half of the 21st Century will be shaped largely by the United States and China. It's in the interests of both countries to avoid confrontation and both countries understand this. Reaching a deal on cyber espionage will help to ensure Sino-American relations remain peaceful.

American-Mexican Relations

America and Mexico have always been linked by geography and are now joined by demographics and economics. Given America's commitment to globalization on other countries' terms, economic disparities between America and Mexico will be narrowed substantially by the middle of this century. This is not a bad thing in of itself, as Mexico is an important American ally, but conservatives should insist that America's trade deficit with her southern neighbor be reduced. NAFTA has not benefited the United States. American corporations that send jobs south of the border should be heavily taxed, and if such taxation is incompatible with NAFTA, then NAFTA should be abolished.

Conclusion

The United States has allowed itself to be led by corporate interests that have hurt the American worker and resulted in massive American trade deficits, which contributed to the Great Recession and near depression. Fealty to globalism has led to diminution of American economic power and contributed to a dwindling military and technology gap between America and China. So long as America puts corporate profits ahead of the national interest, the United States will continue to participate in economic and national security self-sabotage.

Chapter 8
Summary

The Republican Party spots Democrats about 240 Electoral College votes from day one of a presidential campaign. Democrats pick up a few states and the White House is theirs. Will the GOP do anything to change this? It's unlikely.

The one thing Republicans are good at is self-destructing. They demographically asphyxiated themselves. Neocons supported the Wall Street casino over Main Street productivity, tax cuts for the rich at the expense of fairness for the American worker, and offshoring over protecting American industry. They spent trillions of dollars on credit card wars. Neoconservatives destroyed the GOP.

It's worth stating just how much neoconservatives have wrecked the GOP. The Republican Party carried 49 states in the 1984 presidential election. Can anyone seriously imagine the GOP winning 49 states again? Why can't the GOP win 49 states again? That Republicans have not asked themselves why they have become so inept in presidential contests (had they asked and answered honestly, Republicans would have adopted some of the ideas in this book) shows a party closed to reality.

Neocons like to say if only people work hard enough, they'll get rich. But plenty of people work hard and don't get rich. Many who got rich were lucky. They were born at the right time in the right place to the right parents, and they met the right people.

Had their circumstances been different, so too would have been their life outcomes.

The 2008 financial crisis exposed finance capitalism as a scam. Too many people were hurt, no one was really punished, and things go on as before. Neocons act as if American workers simply got in the way of the casino and "the market is always right," and are the real villains. Not acceptable.

What to Do?

1) Conservatives should support evidence-based policymaking. Contempt for reason and evidence among dogma-driven elites harms society. People outside groupthink political parties and groupthink media understand good ideas exist in divergent parts of the political spectrum. In so far as dogma exists in all ideologies, espousing an evidence-based ideology is itself a form of dogma, but if dogma is ubiquitous then surely it makes sense to have it correspond with reality. *In short, go with the evidence, and go with what works!*

Most people agree the rich should pay their fair share of taxes. Many of the same people agree that moderate immigration makes more sense than mass immigration. These are not right or left perspectives, but common sense, based on the evidence.

Members of political parties are more likely to be dogmatic than the general population. Commitment to ideological purity is a reason many people join a political party in the first place. Adherence to ideology often results in poor governance as no ideology has all the right answers. One of the most important attributes any politician can have is an iconoclastic disposition. Liberals and neocons are largely incapable of such an outlook, preferring to check off boxes to make sure they have conformed to being good liberals or good neocons. Such political infantilism is rampant in the United States. Politicians who challenge the dogma of their party are few and far between in the United States, and this goes a long way in explaining much of America's political divide.

2) Conservatives need to accept that the Republican Party has a problem with white voters. It's a greater problem than the one the GOP has with Latinos. For all the Republican handwringing at being unable to win Latino voters, that problem is moot if the GOP keeps losing Ohio, Pennsylvania, Wisconsin, and other northern states.

Blacks, Latinos, and Asians vote overwhelmingly Democratic. Anglo-American evangelicals, southern British Americans, and white Mormons vote heavily Republican. White ethnics switch back in forth, having voted for Woodrow Wilson, FDR, Kennedy, Clinton, and Obama, and also for Theodore Roosevelt, Eisenhower, Nixon, and Reagan.

The white ethnic vote is a vote in play, about the only vote in play. White ethnics give both parties a chance. To its detriment, the GOP has taken for granted white ethnics and the northern white working class. To ignore the interests of one's base doesn't make for winning politics. Republicans are right to worry about their poor showing among Latinos, but millions fewer whites voted in Election 2012 than in 2008 despite an increase in the white voting population. The GOP seems not to care.

European Americans have responded in kind by not caring about the GOP.

Many whites feel neither party represents them. They see a Democratic Party that caters to a Wall Street/Academia/ and Hollywood faction of liberal political donors, and a GOP that defends globalism, war, and corporate privilege. But if given a choice between voting for Democrats or Republicans, many working class whites will opt for the Democratic Party and this will likely remain the case so long as the GOP remains committed to pampering the rich.

Future presidential campaigns by conservatives must be centered on the middle and working classes. Completely. Totally. For all of the political strategists at their disposable, Republicans have yet to figure this out.

3) Conservatives need to adopt an economic policy of moderate and effective government to gain confidence of white and Latino voters. A philosophy of "small government" doesn't resonate with the American electorate and large government risks bankrupting the country. Government can do some things better than the private sector, including healthcare. This is reality. Conservatives shouldn't try to give reality a bloody nose. It has a habit of smacking back.

4) Protect American jobs. Impose tariffs on most foreign goods, thereby cutting back on imports and creating conditions for a manufacturing surge. Tariffs would help eliminate the trade deficit, grow the economy, and reduce unemployment. But the United States should maintain free trade with Canada, as part

of a commitment to an Anglosphere Common Market in North America.

Many people are poor because government refused to step up to the bat for them, doing nothing to stop decent-paying jobs from being sent overseas. Opposition to globalization must be a central tenet of a conservative political platform.

Reestablishing the primacy of industrial capitalism over finance capitalism will help assuage the cynicism of people who see the Wall Street-Washington Axis as an organized crime ring protected by the feds.

Supporting the establishment of a Department of Science and Industry, so as to coordinate government and industry to develop and build cutting edge products in America, is to value honest work and productive economic practices. America will then be able to better compete against China's state capitalism.

Medium and large-sized corporations should include worker representatives on their corporate boards or adopt a two-tier board system, akin to the German corporate structure, whereby a supervisory board consisting of employee representatives must give support to many decisions taken by the management board for those decisions to come into effect. This gives workers a say in wage structures, work conditions, and offshoring.

5) Adopt a 40 percent tax rate on individual income over $80,000, and on family income over $140,000. Adopt a 47 percent tax rate on individual income over $140,000, and on family income over $200,000. Increase the tax rate to 60 percent on individual or family income above $300,000. Individuals making

under $25,000 should be exempt from paying income taxes, as should families making under $35,000.

In the spirit of fairness, and to advance social harmonization, impose a 1 percent wealth tax on individual assets above $50 million, and a 3 percent wealth tax on individual assets above $200 million. Coddling the rich is an idea whose time is over.

Capital gains should be taxed at a rate of 40 percent once an individual has made more than $10 million in the casino.

Corporate tax rates should decrease to 10 percent for companies that maintain primary manufacturing operations in America and rise to 60 percent on investment banks and companies that maintain significant manufacturing operations abroad. It's antithetical to a sound U.S. economy that the financial sector accounts for almost half of U.S. domestic corporate profits and that many American companies assemble most of their products abroad.

Investment banks should each year be required to write checks, amounting to one-third of their profits, to working and middle class Americans. If the banks plead hardship, they should feel free to end annual bonuses to bank employees and take other measures to ensure a friendly orientation toward American workers.

Despite trillions having being spent, the war on poverty has had a mixed record. The poor have benefited from social programs in that most poor Americans have a roof over their head and food, but the gap between rich and poor remains large, and many in the middle class are struggling pay check to pay check.

The measures in this book are designed to transfer some of the responsibility of helping the poor from government to the private sector, but tax policy remains an area where government can bring more fairness to society. A more balanced approach to poverty alleviation bolsters the idea of America as a communitarian society, of the idea that everyone is in it together. Corporations have to stop thinking in terms of maximizing wealth for shareholders, but instead focus on creating good-paying jobs for American workers.

Individual behavior plays a role in the cycle of poverty. Having children out of wedlock is not a good thing and proportionately more children are now born out of wedlock than ever before, although birth rates have fallen for all racial groups, so single mothers have fewer out of wedlock children.

Most of the poor try to help themselves as best they can. But it was government and business that worked to deconstruct the U.S. economy, making sure there would be fewer opportunities for American workers, and government and business made possible the Great Recession. Government and business now have a duty to help the poor.

6) Cutting spending is part of the deficit-fighting equation, but a large part of the debt can be blamed on low economic growth and excessive medical costs of an inefficient healthcare system. Growing the economy at more than 3 percent per annum, which has historically been normal after recessions, would reduce the deficit and ultimately the debt.

Bringing healthcare costs down from 17.5-18 percent of GDP to 12-13 percent would save hundreds of billions of dollars a year. Defense and foreign aid spending can be cut, and so can spending on various government departments and agencies. Government salaries can be cut to private sector levels. These steps should result in an additional $100-$150 billion in savings.

Another major reason for America's debt, a weak economy, can be remedied by tariffs and a hybrid private enterprise/state capitalist economy.

7) Conservatives should demand big banks undergo a government audit and then a second audit by an independent accounting firm, monitored by outside observers. Current auditors have relationships with banks that go back years and decades. After the audits, nationalize and break up the banks. Limit bank leverage, making it mandatory for banks to use more of their own money for business. Bank executives should be held personally accountable for transactions that cripple the economy and face stiff jail terms. Many things have discredited laissez faire, including the practice of investment bankers rolling the dice and not being punished for economic havoc.

Institute a rigorous but simple regulatory process for the banks. Glass-Steagall took up 37 pages while Dodd-Frank is a jumble of far greater length. Eliminate loopholes that allow investment banks to roll the dice and wreck the country. End quantitative easing.

8) Conservatives need to support a state-managed national healthcare policy. If the Affordable Care Act doesn't result in considerable savings, healthcare should be nationalized. A parallel private system can

exist alongside a public one to prevent the public one from being overburdened.

9) Reduce immigration to 200,000-400,000 immigrants a year in order to put upward pressure on wages and provide more opportunities for American workers. Allow free movement of labor between Canada and the United States.

Securing America's southern border should have happened decades ago. Not securing the border ranks among the great failings of American history. That America has spent trillions fighting overseas wars, but has refused to spend a fraction of that amount to defend its own border is an affront to reason.

10) Increase the minimum wage to $14 an hour over several years. What is the point of earning a wage if one can't live on it? Conservatives need to understand this and act accordingly.

11) Extend unemployment benefits to at least three years. The unemployed need to be given a safety cushion and shouldn't suffer because political elites value Wall Street over Main Street.

12) Support gay marriage. Gays should have all the rights and responsibilities accorded to heterosexuals.

13) Gun violence in America has fallen steadily for decades. Conservatives should support outlawing assault weapons, but gun legislation should be the responsibility of the states. Institute stiff penalties for gun crimes.

14) Extend affirmative action to white ethnics, gay white men, transgendered individuals, introverts, older workers, and poor British-Americans. Doing so will build a more inclusive society.

15) Adopt a harm reduction approach to drug addiction. Locking up people because they're addicted to illegal substances is immoral.

16) Legalize prostitution for gay men. It should be regulated, but not criminalized. Some feminists want to outlaw the buying of sexual services, and if it involves a man wanting to buy sex from a woman, that's fine. But this approach imposes feminist standards on gay men for whom the cultural and power dynamics of prostitution differ from feminist perspectives. Gay men have the right to do what they want with their bodies and not have that right undermined by feminist or heteronormative values.

17) Protect free speech. Oppose legislation/policies/pressures/fads designed to repress political opinions and political speech.

18) A conservative party should be an ideas party, a party with vision. Neocon policies lead to dystopian outcomes. Workers succumb to the casino. Soldiers die in endless wars. American jobs belong in China. This doesn't win votes.

19) Adopt a realist foreign policy, not a foreign policy based on permanent war and bankrupting America. It shouldn't be necessary to state the obvious, but it's a good idea not to attack countries that haven't attacked you or your allies.

20) Invest in infrastructure and jobs training programs. America's infrastructure is crumbling. It will have to be fixed regardless of economic conditions. Millions of infrastructure jobs can be created over the next thirty years. Developing a green economy will also help reduce unemployment.

21) Invest in public relations and communications. Conservatives are going to need to get an appealing message across to the many groups who are currently suspicious, if not outright hostile, to the GOP.

22) Support the welfare state. This includes state healthcare, social assistance of various types, including disability payments, housing support, and food stamps. Social program costs will fall if the minimum wage is increased to $14 an hour and if a Guaranteed Basic Income is introduced. Government has the moral obligation to look out for its citizens, not bash them. Opposing the welfare state while offshoring jobs, keeping wages low, and supporting mass immigration is as irrational as it is immoral.

Republicans have scared away too many people, and whatever reservations voters have about Democrats these concerns aren't as great as the loathing the working class has developed for the GOP.

23) Conservatives should advocate taxing oil and gas company profits at 50-60 percent, using some of the money to establish an energy trust fund, which would pay out a yearly check to working and middle class Americans. A separate energy trust fund should be established to help keep Social Security solvent.

24) Go negative in presidential campaigns. Many lessons came out of Election 2012. It demonstrated the ineffectiveness of the Republican candidate and message. It also showed that negative campaigning works in spades.

25) Get rid of the Electoral College. Of all the ways to elect a president, the Electoral College ranks among the silliest. Have a straight-up vote. The candidate with the most votes wins. Every vote will count

whereas now it makes no sense for a California conservative to vote for president. In a contest where no candidate gets 50 percent of the vote, consider having a run-off.

Chapter 9
America to 2050

Historically speaking, it hasn't been a good idea to bet against America, but today's country is not the confident and cohesive society of the past, where adversity was seen as a challenge that would be overcome, and where American government and business were committed to advancing America, not advancing China. Instead, the United States is mired in a victimization mindset and a corporate globalist agenda that gives claims of victimization credence. It's a downward spiral, and for the former to end, the latter must end.

Oil and natural gas finds combined with new energy extraction technologies and green energy will mean America will be energy self-sufficient by 2030. North Dakota is sometimes called America's Kuwait and California might be America's Saudi Arabia. There could be enough shale oil reserves in the Golden State to turbocharge California's economic growth for decades.

If America's energy boom is managed right, a trust fund will be established to help keep Social Security viable for the rest of this century. America's energy rush could help drive the stock market higher in coming years, but the poor don't have money to buy stocks and yet again will be left out in the cold by a government determined to rig things in favor of the rich. Quantitative easing might have set the stage for another market bubble if economic growth remains weak.

Reshoring of manufacturing because of rising wages in China and cheap energy at home could balance out or exceed offshoring by the 2020s. New jobs will be created in factories and throughout the manufacturing supply chain. This won't be a repeat of the 20th Century manufacturing boom because offshoring will still occur and robots and automation processes will be prevalent on the factory floor.

Within three decades, robots and AI will do most repetitive work, general labor and white-collar jobs. New types of jobs will be created and machines will do most of them as well. Humans will have to find employment niches for themselves and self-employment will skyrocket.

It's possible that productivity gains of robotized workplaces in combination with America's energy reserves and development of new technologies will allow government to pay for an extensive safety net and a Guaranteed Basic Income so that work is an option, not a necessity. Corporations will be taxed heavily in a robot-dominated era. Robots might liberate human beings, eliminating the need to work, allowing people to engage in personally meaningful pursuits.

By 2050, the average lifespan in the United States will be at least three years longer than today and cancer and heart disease will be curable or manageable. A human zygote/embryo-selection, genomic-enhancement, cybernetic-augmentation race between nations is possible. If one nation adopts human enhancement technologies, other countries will follow.

A threat to American internal stability is the rigged structural nature of American inequality. These structural barriers need to be torn down. Disconnect between the real economy and Wall Street owing to a rigged casino increases the odds of conflict in the United States. Wall Street privilege exacerbates socioeconomic divisions. If American elites continue to be indifferent to the hardships of ordinary people, an American Spring is possible.

Liberal and neocon elites have for decades pushed a globalist agenda on American workers, who for decades have been treated with contempt. From their comfortable homes in well-heeled suburbs, the elites seem not to care that there is only so much that ordinary people can take.

Possibly a few neocons and libertarians, sensing defeat, delve ever deeper into libertarian texts to see if they have somehow misinterpreted some quote or other of one of their heroes. Perhaps, they conclude, America's economic difficulties are the result of not enough free trade, and that America's trade deficits just weren't large enough. These globalist fanatics are as blind to reality as the Soviet Politburo was in the 1980s.

This raises philosophical questions about the nature of American government: Why did it permit American deindustrialization in the name of "free trade?" Why did it do nothing as financial gangsters wrought the Great Recession? Why were those responsible not punished? How can it consider giving amnesty to more than ten million people and dramatically hiking legal immigration without increasing the minimum wage to $14 an hour? Why is it so obsessed with pampering the super rich? Is being in the good graces of corporate executives and investment bankers really worth the destruction of a country?

Political division could sabotage economic growth. Two polarizing political groups have political voice in America, a laissez-faire globalist one, and a left-wing globalist one. Both excel at playing *race to the bottom*. Neither Democrats nor Republicans stand with the American worker and the realist right and center have little voice in Washington. This might change if the GOP implodes in the next two decades. A good scenario would see new parties take as many votes away from Democrats as from the GOP, allowing for political realignment that benefits the middle class and poor.

America contains multiple ethnic groups, but it is defined by a dominant culture, the English one that made America and the U.S. Constitution possible. Having one leading culture has brought unity to an otherwise diverse country. Future American leaders would be wise to remember America's unofficial motto of *E Pluribus Unum*.

One can always start a discussion on political philosophy with a statement: There are no good dictators. If America becomes a de facto one-party state, it would not be too far-fetched to see things formalized, but it's also possible that technological advances combined with economic/military rivalry with China or concerns over terrorism could lead to the balance between privacy and security being skewed toward security. "Security" might then become a reason to diminish liberty in order to pursue "domestic terrorists."

In a surveillance state, people could be reminded of their vulnerability through subtle psychological manipulation, resulting in behavior modification. Such a PSYOP, conducted over many years, could induce in people a mental state associated with living in a police state. Soft totalitarianism would amplify cognitive dissonance, as the government would insist it was a *democracy*, the word losing any association with *liberty*.

Unless the business cycle has been repealed, a depression is likely before 2050. America has experienced 47 or so recessions since 1790 and several depressions. But the main reason a depression is likely is because America has learned little from the Great Recession. Insiders are as tightly in charge of the U.S. economy as ever and new financial sector "regulations" are so full of loopholes that Wall Street continues in its toxic ways with impunity.

The next depression will be different from previous ones for several reasons. It will be the first depression to occur with a large portion of Americans dependent on government. Second, America's debt-to-GDP ratio is much higher than it was at the onset of the Great Depression in 1930. Budget deficits, although shrinking, are likely to continue for the rest of this decade. Third, in the 1930s many people still lived on farms or had relatives who did so. As poor as people were then, many folks had access to food that didn't involve paying for it at a supermarket. Fourth, America is today a more heterogeneous society than it was in the 1930s and there is little agreement on many of the issues of the day.

Energy wealth in combination with machine-generated productivity gains might make even a depression a relatively minor event. The last depression spurred creation of pensions and government programs and since then the welfare state has been growing and rightfully so.

In any increasingly complex system there is an increased chance that something might go wrong. As the world becomes more complex, and if American government and business wage war against the American worker, more welfare provisions will be needed. A living wage and Guaranteed Basic Income will become civil rights issues in coming years.

The long-term viability of Social Security will have to be addressed over the next two decades with eligibility levels indexed to reflect increased life expectancies and growing income inequalities. In addition to tapping into energy wealth to finance Social Security, government should, within a generation, use energy money to fund robot companions for poor elderly Americans.

America will retain the benefit of two strengths. The first is energy and food self-sufficiency. The country will likely remain self-sufficient in water, although the depletion of the Ogallala Aquifer might lead to desertification of parts of the Great Plains.

America's other great strength is the creativity of her people. Although the United States lags behind Switzerland, Germany, Sweden, Japan, Denmark, and Finland in terms of patents filed per million people, America still files more than a quarter of all patents in the world and wins a large percentage of Nobel Prizes. Creativity in combination with entrepreneurial drive and capital have been among America's greatest strengths and will remain key to American success in this century.

Conclusion

The 2028 presidential election will be the GOP's last kick at the can if the party doesn't change its ways. If the GOP combines different conservative strands into a realist platform the party might yet win an election or two without requiring a black swan event to salvage it. If the Republican Party can nominate candidates who combine common sense policies with populist appeal, and who focus all of their efforts on the middle and working classes, the GOP's expiration date could be pushed further into the future.

America's economic paradigm is centered on ensuring corporate profit margins become bigger, corporate executives become richer, and American workers become poorer. America no longer has a market economy serving the national interest, but a racket benefiting the wealthy. The GOP either stops defending a globalist corporate agenda or the Republican Party is done.

Nowhere on the horizon is there a prominent Republican with the right political stuff. To make yet another neocon the Republican presidential candidate would be a farce. What would be the point of it?

An ideal conservative presidential candidate will embrace realist conservatism, which means a paleocon immigration policy, realpolitik foreign policy, libertarian social policy, and progressive conservative tax and healthcare policies. Free enterprise would mix with state capitalism. As of the time of this writing, the Republican Party is too dogmatic to think outside a crumpled neocon box.

Tea Party or social conservative types who believe there exists mass support for a Tea Party presidential candidate are deluding themselves. It would take recession and an Obamacare disaster to elect a Tea Party president. Possible but unlikely.

The country's demographics have changed, as has the culture. People are more socially liberal than 30 years ago, mainly because they see through the hypocrisy of social conservatism. Many children of Reagan Democrats support gay marriage. So do many aging Reagan Democrats. Nor is bashing the poor a vote winner, partly because people see Wall Street receiving trillions in welfare. The other reason bashing the poor is not a vote winner is because so many working people are only a few paychecks away from poverty.

The Tea Party has largely been a movement against Democrats and against government. But to win the presidency, it's not enough to be against government. Ideas that don't involve tearing down government have to be offered.

The current Republican Party is rotted to the core. If it weren't rotted to the core, it would never have allowed a fringe group, the neocons, to take it over so totally. Historians will ask how a small group of globalist fanatics were allowed to destroy the Party of Lincoln. And why did conservatives allow it to happen? Conservative suicide will be the subject of future academic dissertations. Mental illness will be much discussed. When one considers the current

Republican Party, one thinks of a drooling man running his finger up and down over his lips. It is to this state that neocons have taken the GOP.

Many investment bankers, private equity consultants, and currency traders believe they deserve their money. They think that somehow they've earned it. With the rules stacked in its favor, Wall Street still plunged America into steep recession, but the folks who made a fortune from the casino can say, "I got mine."

Conservatives need to make American workers the central part of their message, not Wall Street greed, not globalism, not dogma or war, but people. If conservatives refuse to stand up for Main Street and American workers, they'll never again win the presidency. Nor would they deserve to.

What will neocons do going forward? Time will tell, but it's easy to imagine one of their number picking up a microphone and announcing, "It's time to play...*race to the bottom*!" Cheers and applause break out from supporters followed by chants of "trickle down, trickle down...!"

A century from now, historians will wonder why a major American political party was so determined to self-destruct.